COUNTRIES OF THE WORLD

Bangladesh

Gareth Stevens Publishing
A WORLD ALMANAC EDUCATION GROUP COMPANY

About the Author: Ellen London lived in Bangladesh for four years with her husband, who is a Medical Officer for the U.S. Peace Corps, and two daughters. London is a qualified librarian and has worked for international schools in Africa and Europe, and as an International Schools Specialist for Ebsco Information Services. Today, she lives with her husband in Bangkok, Thailand, but continues to travel frequently to Bangladesh.

Acknowledgements: The publishers would like to thank Mohammad Shams-Ul Islam, CEO/Director of Agrani Exchange House Private Limited (An Exchange House owned by AGRANI BANK, Bangladesh), for the loan and use of his samples of Bangladeshi currency in this book.

PICTURE CREDITS
Agence France Presse: 14, 15 (bottom), 17, 27 (top), 36, 37, 38, 47, 56, 57, 72, 73, 74, 75, 77, 78, 79, 81, 83
Art Directors & TRIP Photo Library: 1, 3 (center and bottom), 4, 5, 8, 9, 11, 12, 19, 21, 26, 27 (bottom), 30, 33, 37, 46, 49, 52, 59, 60, 62, 63, 64, 65, 68, 69 (top), 80
Bes Stock: 66, 87
CCP, Courtesy of Photoshare: 82
Haga Library, Japan: 3 (top), 31
HBL Network Photo Agency: 76
Hutchison Picture Library: cover, 6, 7, 24, 32, 42, 43, 45, 53, 58, 67, 91
Jason Laure: 20, 54, 55, 70, 71 (top and bottom), 84
Ellen London: 28, 35, 69 (bottom)
Lonely Planet Images: 18
David Simson: 2, 22, 40, 41, 48
Liba Taylor: 23, 25, 34, 44, 61, 89
Topham Picturepoint: 13, 16, 29, 50, 51, 85

Digital Scanning by Superskill Graphics Pte Ltd

Written by
ELLEN LONDON

Edited by
CHARISSA MARIE NAIR

Edited in the U.S. by
RICHARD SWETALLA
ALAN WACHTEL

Designed by
JAILANI BASARI

Picture research by
SUSAN JANE MANUEL

First published in North America in 2004 by
Gareth Stevens Publishing
A World Almanac Education Group Company
330 West Olive Street, Suite 100
Milwaukee, Wisconsin 53212 USA

Please visit our web site at
www.garethstevens.com
For a free color catalog describing
Gareth Stevens Publishing's list of
high-quality books and multimedia programs,
call 1-800-542-2595 (USA) or 1-800-387-3178 (Canada).
Gareth Stevens Publishing's fax: (414) 332-3567.

© **TIMES MEDIA PRIVATE LIMITED 2004**
Originated and designed by
Times Editions
An imprint of Times Media Private Limited
A member of the Times Publishing Group
Times Centre, 1 New Industrial Road
Singapore 536196
http://www.timesone.com.sg/te

Library of Congress Cataloging-in-Publication Data
London, Ellen.
Bangladesh / Ellen London.
p. cm. — (Countries of the world)
Summary: Provides an overview of the geography, history, government, language, art, and food of Bangladesh, exploring its customs and current issues.
Includes bibliographical references and index.
ISBN 0-8368-3107-1 (lib. bdg.)
1. Bangladesh—Juvenile literature. [1. Bangladesh.]
I. Title. II. Countries of the world (Milwaukee, Wis.)
DS393.4.L66   2004
954.92—dc22   2003057394

Printed in Singapore

1 2 3 4 5 6 7 8 9 08 07 06 05 04

Contents

AN OVERVIEW OF BANGLADESH

Bangladesh is one of the world's poorest and most densely populated countries. Bangladeshis form the world's second-largest Muslim population, and Islam is the state religion. Flood plains cover most of the country's area, and with about 5,000 miles (8,045 kilometers) of waterways in Bangladesh, boats are a major means of transportation for the country's people. A subtropical climate and frequent monsoon rains support Bangladesh's lush plant life. The Sundarbans, the world's longest mangrove belt, span most of the country's southern border. Bangladesh is also home to the endangered Royal Bengal tiger. A young nation, Bangladesh became independent only in 1971, after it won the Liberation War, its war for independence from West Pakistan.

Opposite: **A statue of three white storks stands outside the Biman Building in Dhaka's business district.**

Below: **Cox's Bazar is a beachside town in southeastern Bangladesh. It is the nearest urban area to the world's longest beach.**

THE FLAG OF BANGLADESH

The national Bangladeshi flag was adopted on January 13, 1972. Bangladesh separated from West Pakistan on March 26, 1971 and officially became an independent nation on December 16, 1971. The flag is green, with a red circle positioned just left of the center of the flag. The red circle symbolizes both the "rising sun of a new country" and the blood shed during Bangladesh's fight for freedom in the Liberation War. The green background is significant for two reasons. First, Islam is the state religion in Bangladesh, and green is the color of Islam. Green is also supposed to represent the rich plant life in the country.

Geography

Located in South Asia, Bangladesh is bordered by India to the west, north, and east, by Myanmar to the southeast, and by the Bay of Bengal to the south. The country covers an area of about 55,584 square miles (144,000 square kilometers) and has a 360-mile (580-km) long coastline. The border Bangladesh shares with India stretches for 2,518 miles (4,053 km), while the border it shares with Myanmar extends for 120 miles (193 km).

The Bangladeshi landscape is mostly uniform, with plains covering more than 90 percent of the country's area. The remaining 10 percent includes lakes, swamps, marshes, and two hilly areas — the Sylhet Hills and the Chittagong Hill Tracts, respectively located in far-northeastern and southeastern Bangladesh. The Chittagong Hill Tracts are a series of low hills that rarely rise above 2,000 feet (610 meters), while the Sylhet Hills range between 100 and 1,100 feet (30 and 335 m) in height. Part of the Chittagong Hill Tracts, Keokradong is the country's highest peak, at 4,036 feet (1,230 m).

A COUNTRY OF RIVERS

Bangladesh is home to many rivers, including the Ganges, the Jamuna, and the Meghna.
(A Closer Look, page 44)

Below: **The city of Dhaka is increasingly overpopulated.**

Bangladesh is home to the world's longest beach, at 75 miles (120 km). Located at Cox's Bazar in southeastern Bangladesh, the beach opens onto the Bay of Bengal. The Sundarbans, a vast mangrove forest, dominates the country's southernmost border.

Flood Plains and Deltas

One of the effects of having three major river systems — the Ganges, Brahmaputra, and Meghna — flowing through the country is that it is divided into numerous deltas and plains. The Barind Tract is a triangular piece of land situated between the Ganges and the Jamuna rivers in northwestern Bangladesh. To the southeast of the Barind Tract, extending for about 100 miles (160 km) to the point where the Ganges and Jamuna rivers meet, lies the Bhar Basin. The Jamuna flood plains are located north of the Bhar Basin and to the east of the Barind Tract. The Madhupur Tract lies in between the Jamuna flood plains to its west and the Northeastern Lowland to its east. The region south of the Jamuna flood plains and the Madhupur Tract in east-central Bangladesh is known as the Meghna Flood Basin. The landscape of southern Bangladesh, the region south of the Ganges river, is dominated by various deltas and is generally known as the Central Delta Basins.

Above: Cox's Bazar has become increasingly popular with tourists in recent years. The country's tourism industry, however, is largely underdeveloped. Although Cox's Bazar's first five-star hotel opened in late 2002, tourists often cannot obtain luxury accommodations or world-class services.

THE SUNDARBANS

Declared a World Heritage Site in 1997 by the United Nations Educational, Scientific, and Cultural Organization (UNESCO), the Sundarbans is part of the world's largest mangrove forest and is located in Bangladesh's Khulna division.

(A Closer Look, page 66)

Six Seasons

Bangladesh has a warm, subtropical climate, with high levels of humidity and frequent thunderstorms. Although Bangladesh is often described as having six seasons — summer; rainy; autumn; late autumn, or misty; winter; and spring — only three are distinctly felt, and they are the winter, summer, and monsoon seasons. Winter, which is mild and humid, lasts from October to March, and January is its coolest month. Summer, which is hot and humid, lasts from March to June. April is the hottest summer month, with maximum temperatures reaching between 91° and 96° Fahrenheit (33° and 36° Celsius). The monsoon season lasts from June to October, and the months of June and July are known as the storm season. Most parts of Bangladesh receive a minimum of about 60 inches (1,524 millimeters) of rainfall a year. Areas in northern, northeastern, southern, and southeastern Bangladesh receive between 80 to 100 inches (2,032 to 2,540 mm) of rain. Especially heavy thunderstorms occur in Bangladesh in the early summer months of April and May and also late in the monsoon season, from September to November. Accompanied by strong winds that blow at more than 100 miles (160 km) per hour, the arrival of these heavy rainstorms often also marks the beginning of a time of devastating tidal waves that rise as high as 20 feet (6 m). The strong winds blowing over the Bay of Bengal cause tidal waves to crash onto the country's southern coastal areas and offshore islands.

Left: Water lilies grow abundantly in bodies of water throughout Bangladesh. The flowers only bloom during the warm months of each year.

Plants and Animals

Plant life in Bangladesh is lush and includes subtropical and tropical species. Forests cover about 15 percent of Bangladesh's area. Trees bearing fruits, such as mangoes, jackfruits, betel nuts, and coconuts, are plentiful in the country, where bamboo and cane also flourish. Bangladesh is also home to a wide variety of flowers, including the *shapla* (SHAH-PLAH), or water lily, which is the national flower of the country. Flowers, such as the marigold; the lotus jasmine; the rajani gandha, which is a type of tuber rose; the jaba, or china rose; and the flame-of-the-forest are common species.

The rich animal life of Bangladesh includes about 200 species of mammals, 750 species of birds, 150 species of reptiles and amphibians, and 200 species of fishes. Elephants and water buffalo are common, as are different kinds of deer. The royal Bengal Tiger, which is indigenous to the Sundarbans, is a rare sight. Bangladesh is also the home of many bears, of which there are three main types — the Himalayan black bear, the Malayan sun bear, and the sloth bear. The rhesus, or Bengal, monkey (*Macaca mulatta*) is common throughout the country and can even be seen resting on concrete walls in the capital city of Dhaka.

BIRDS OF BANGLADESH

Bird life in Bangladesh is remarkably diverse and includes beautiful species such as the bulbul and the magpie robin. Mynah birds, cuckoos, parakeets, and woodpeckers are some of the more common species. Birds of prey include owls, hawks, and vultures. Bangladesh is also home to several species of eagles, including the ring-tailed fishing eagle and the crested serpent eagle. Herons, storks, ducks, and wild geese are not unusual in the country.

History

The earliest known inhabitants of the land that is Bangladesh today were a tribe of Dravidian-speaking people who would later become known as the Bang. They are believed to have occupied Bengal, an area consisting of the current Bangladesh and the Indian state of West Bengal, from as early as 1000 B.C.

The Subject of Successive Empires

The Mauryan Empire (c. 320–180 B.C.) was the first to unite the region consisting of present-day India, Pakistan, and Bangladesh. As the empire declined, eastern Bengal (now Bangladesh) became the kingdom of Samatata, an independent division within the Gupta Empire (c. A.D. 319–540) of India. Eastern Bengal remained largely neglected under the Harsha Empire (606–647), which gave way to the Pala Dynasty (750–1150). Buddhist chief Gopala united Bengal and was the first of the Pala rulers who provided the people with prolonged peace and prosperity. Under the Palas, Buddhism spread throughout the land. In 1150, the Senas, a group of militant, orthodox Hindus, conquered Bengal and imposed an oppressive caste system that divided the people into various upper and lower classes. Near the end of the 1100s, the Senas were overthrown by Turkish warriors, who had earlier conquered much of the Indian subcontinent including present-day Afghanistan. Although the last Sena ruler was overthrown in 1202, a few Sena leaders managed to uphold a brief resistance in eastern Bengal outside the Sena capital of Nadia in western Bengal. Under the Turks, most people in Bengal converted to Islam.

The Delhi Sultanate (1206–1526)

For over a century, the Delhi Sultanate exercised some influence over Bengal. The sultanate began as a Muslim territory in northern India, including present-day Pakistan, and gradually expanded. In Bengal, the sultanate demanded tributes of war elephants in exchange for administrative autonomy. In 1341, the sultanate lost control of Bengal, and Dhaka, in eastern Bengal, became the new center of government. Before the Mughals arrived in the late 1500s, the Turks managed to wrestle Bengal from its governors for several decades.

THE MUGHALS

The Mughal Empire began in 1526 but did not include Bengal until 1576, when Dhaka was captured by the armies of Emperor Akbar the Great (*top row, center*).

Under the Mughals, Bengal's role in the empire as the "bread basket of India" led to increased agricultural production and income, but its resources were drained to support the Mughal army. Bengal was also left undefended against pirates, who were kidnapping up to 40,000 Bengalis a year to serve as slaves elsewhere. Pockets of resistance began emerge but were swiftly quashed by mighty Mughal generals sent to Bengal to serve as governors. Despite the instability, trade in Bengal thrived, and Dhaka became a major textile center in South Asia.

Centralized Mughal power waned after Emperor Aurangzeb died in 1707, and his successors failed to regain any real control over the individual governors. Bengal, in particular, was so self-reliant that it successfully defended itself against an invasion by the Hindu Marathas. In 1757, however, Siraj ud Daulah, Bengal's governor at that time, provoked a battle against British forces, to whom he lost Bengal.

THE GREAT MUTINY OF 1857

The East India Company was profiting handsomely from exploiting the subcontinent's rich resources but showed little concern for the locals, who were becoming increasingly unhappy. Anti-British sentiment among the people culminated in the Great Mutiny of 1857, which prompted the British government to intervene. By June 1858, the last of the rebel groups surrendered and Emperor Bahadur Shah was exiled to Burma (now Myanmar), marking the formal end of the Mughal Empire.

The Rise of British Rule

Although European traders had been visiting the Indian subcontinent since the fifth century B.C., European settlement only began in the late 1400s. European, especially British, presence and influence rose as the Mughal Empire declined.

Established in 1600, the East India Company, with the support of the British government, first went to South Asia with the intention of persuading local Mughal governors to enter into trade agreements that gave the company special rights. In the 1600s, the company built a factory on the Hooghly River and founded the city of Calcutta in western Bengal. After winning the battle at Plassey in 1757, the company gained a base in Bengal, from which it gradually expanded its territorial claims. By the 1850s, the company controlled an area roughly consisting of present-day India, Pakistan, and Bangladesh and held unparalleled power throughout the land. The Mughals, nevertheless, were officially in power until 1858, when the British government dissolved the East India Company and took direct control of the company's territory, which the government renamed "British India."

India underwent tremendous change in the latter half of the 1800s. An educational system modeled after that of the British and extensive transportation and communication infrastructure were introduced. The economy of British India boomed as a result of international trade.

BRITISH INDIA DIVIDED

While known as British India, western Bengal developed more rapidly than eastern Bengal, which remained largely agricultural. Religion also separated Bengal's east from its west. The people of western Bengal were mostly Hindus, while the people of eastern Bengal tended to be Muslims. Hindus were more likely to be British-educated.

Partition and Two Pakistans

In 1947, Britain divided British India into two independent countries — India and Pakistan, which consisted of both the eastern- and westernmost sections of the territory. East Pakistan (now Bangladesh) was separated from West Pakistan (now Pakistan) by the width of India, which is about 1,000 miles (1,600 km) wide. The people of East and West Pakistan may have shared the same religion — Islam — but their mother tongues and cultures differed greatly. West Pakistan also controlled the newly formed state's government, economy, and military, even though more than half of its population lived in East Pakistan. Relations between East and West Pakistan were uneasy from the start and grew increasingly strained after the national government based in West Pakistan declared Urdu the country's official language. The decision sparked much civil fighting and unrest in East Pakistan, where most people spoke Bangla.

THE FIRST TRY AT PARTITION

In 1905, the British, at the recommendation of Lord George Cuzon, divided Bengal into two provinces — West Bengal (now the Indian state of West Bengal) and Eastern Bengal and Assam (now Bangladesh and the Indian state of Assam). Cuzon's move greatly angered upper-class Hindus, who saw it as a threat to their power, but was welcomed by many Muslims as recognition of their religious and political differences. A group of Hindu politicians from India then launched a nationalistic campaign, which Calcutta's Hindu elite supported, to topple Cuzon, and the division was reversed in 1912. Tensions between Bengal's Hindus and Muslims grew fiery and spread throughout India. Sustained conflict between the two groups led the British to believe that Hindus and Muslims needed to be separated into two countries.

Left: These ethnic Bengalis are making tea boxes under the direct supervision of a British official. Before partition, the British were actively involved in Bengal's economy. After partition, Bengal's economy became controlled by West Pakistan.

Left: Bangladeshi president Iajuddin Ahmed (*left*), Sri Lankan president Chandrika Kumaratunga (*center*), and Bangladeshi prime minister Begum Khaleda Zia (*right*) wave to members of the press. President Kumaratunga was in Dhaka for a two-day visit in April 2003. She was the first Sri Lankan leader to visit Bangladesh in eight years.

The Liberation War and After

Two decades of political power struggles between the two Pakistans finally erupted on March 25, 1971, when the Pakistan Army descended on East Pakistan and began a nine-month killing spree. This violent move was aimed at crushing East Pakistan's ambition for self-government, and it made an enemy of India, which openly condemned the mindless slaughter of hundreds of thousands of Bengalis. On December 4, 1971, India entered Bangladesh's war for independence, and the Pakistan Army officially surrendered in less than two weeks, on December 16.

Sheikh Mujib was named Bangladesh's first president while in exile in April 1971. He was a political prisoner in Pakistan at that time and was freed in January 1972 under the watchful eyes of the international community. In 1973, Mujib's political party, the Awami League, won the country's first general elections in a landslide victory. Mujib was assassinated, however, in 1975, and martial law was declared during the period of chaos that followed. Major Ziaur Rahman, known to locals as Zia, took control of the country in 1976. President Zia, leader of the Bangladesh National Party (BNP), was assassinated in 1981, and Vice President Abdus Sattar was later elected president of Bangladesh. In 1982, Lieutenant General Hussain Muhammad Ershad forcibly took control of the country and ruled until 1990. Bangladeshis, however, resented Ershad's iron-fisted rule and regarded his position of power as unrightfully gained. In 1990, Ershad resigned because of mass protests against him in the country.

AN INFLUENTIAL LEADER

Bangladesh's early years were fraught with power struggles and civil strife. Widely regarded as the founding father of Bangladesh, Sheikh Mujib, along with twelve members of his family, was killed on August 15, 1975, in a violent military coup. (*A Closer Look, page 54*)

WOMEN IN POLITICS

After Ershad, Bangladesh's political scene has been dominated by two high-profile women — Begum Khaleda Zia, the widow of assasinated President Zia, and Sheikh Hasina Wajed, daughter of Sheikh Mujib. In 1991, Khaleda Zia became Bangladesh's first female prime minister.

Asoka (273–232 B.C.)

The most famous of all Mauryan rulers, Asoka was very brutal during the early years of his rule. After conquering most of the Indian subcontinent, however, Asoka decided to abandon his violent side and follow Buddhism instead. The teachings of the religion, which encourage kindness and compassion, greatly influenced Asoka's later reign. Because the Mauryan Empire became a place of peace and pacifism, invaders took the opportunity to destroy the empire. Today, Asoka is fondly remembered for building hospitals dedicated to saving animals, among other kind deeds. Asoka also left a rich legacy of carved inscriptions that preserved and promoted Buddhist principles.

Akbar the Great (1556–1605)

The most revered of the Mughal emperors, Akbar the Great was the grandson of Zahir-ud-Din Muhammad Babur, the founder of the empire and a descendant of Genghis Khan. Akbar ascended to the throne when he was thirteen years old and went on to control most of northern and central India. An insightful and enlightened ruler, Akbar was a strong defender of justice and religious tolerance. He believed in equal rights for all men regardless of race or religion and lifted Mughal civilization to new heights. Akbar's unbiased approach allowed him to unite an otherwise deeply divided population and, with that unity, build a mighty and prosperous kingdom.

Sheikh Hasina Wajed (1947–)

The daughter of Sheikh Mujib, Sheikh Hasina Wajed became Bangladesh's second female prime minister in 1996. Although she was forced into exile after her father and family were killed in 1975, Sheikh Hasina was elected president of the Awami League in 1981 and returned to Bangladesh. For two terms, beginning in 1986 and 1991, she led the Awami League, the opposition party in Bangladesh's parliament. Between 1994 and 1996, her party launched a campaign that led Prime Minister Khaleda Zia to resign in March 1996. Three months later, the Awami League won the parliamentary majority, and Sheikh Hasina became prime minister. In the 2001 elections, she lost to Khaleda Zia.

Sheikh Hasina Wajed

Government and the Economy

A Parliamentary Democracy

The Bangladeshi government is made up of three main branches — executive, legislative, and judicial. The executive branch is led more by the prime minister than the president, whose duties are largely ceremonial, unless parliament is dissolved and an interim, or caretaker, government is established. The Bangladeshi president is elected by members of parliament to serve a five-year term, while the prime minister is appointed by the president. The prime minister is usually the leader of the political party that won the greatest number of seats in parliament. The prime minister is assisted by a cabinet of ministers, who are selected by the prime minister and appointed by the president.

Below: **Bangladesh's parliament building was designed by American architect Louis Isadore Khan (1901–1974).**

Left: **Bangladeshi president Iajuddin Ahmed (*left*), Navy Chief Admiral Shah Iqbal Muztaba (*center*), Air Force Chief Vice Marshal Fakhru Azam (*right*), and Army Chief Lieutenant General Hasah Mashhud (*left, in background*) stand at attention for the ceremony marking Bangladesh's 2003 Independence Day.**

The legislative branch in Bangladesh consists of a unicameral, or one-house, parliament, known as the Jatiya Sangsad, or National Parliament. The National Parliament is composed of 300 members, all of whom are popularly elected to serve five-year terms. Following the October 2001 elections, the Bangladesh Nationalist Party (BNP), Jamaat-i-Islami (JI), Islami Okiya Jote (IOJ), and Jatiya Party (JP) joined forces to form a coalition that makes up the country's parliamentary majority.

The judiciary of Bangladesh is based on the English common law system. Under the common law system, judges are required to follow case precedents set by those serving in the country's higher courts. The Supreme Court is the country's highest court and oversees a system of lower courts, including those in the High Court Division and the Appellate Division. The judges are appointed by the president.

Local Government

Bangladesh is divided into six administrative regions, and they are Rajshahi, Khulna, Dhaka, Barisal, Chittagong, and Sylhet. Each division is divided into different *zilla* (JEH-lah), or districts, which are further divided into 460 *thana* (THAH-nah), or groups of villages. Each thana is headed by an executive officer, whose responsibilities include administrative and judicial duties. The village is the smallest unit of local government.

MILITARY

The Bangladeshi military divides into an army; navy; air force; coast guard; and paramilitary forces, including the Bangladesh Rifles, Bangladesh Ansars, Village Defense Parties, Armed Police Battalions, and National Cadet Corps. In 2002, more than 22 million male Bangladeshis were considered fit for military service.

Economy

Bangladesh suffers from a workforce that is growing too rapidly for the number of jobs available in the country. As a result, more and more Bangladeshis have been leaving the country each year to find work elsewhere. Countries such as Saudi Arabia, Kuwait, Singapore, and Malaysia are hosts to significant populations of Bangladeshi workers. In 2001, the unemployment rate in Bangladesh was estimated at 35 percent.

In 2000, the service sector of Bangladesh's economy provided 52 percent of the country's gross domestic product (GDP). Its agricultural sector contributed 30 percent and its industrial sector contributed 18 percent. Today, Bangladesh's most important natural resources are its abundant fertile soil and its natural gas and petroleum reserves. Natural gas and petroleum are not yet exploited as export products.

Agriculture

About two-thirds of the Bangladeshi workforce are employed in the agricultural sector, and most of the food produced is used to feed the country's people. Bangladeshi farmers mainly grow rice, jute, tea, wheat, sugarcane, potatoes, legumes, spices, and various

NATURAL GAS

Bangladesh has large reserves of natural gas. Despite the potential of natural gas as a lucrative export product, the Bangladeshi government is cautious in deciding what to do with the country's valuable resources. India, for example, has shown keen interest in buying gas exports from Bangladesh, but Bangladesh wants to make sure that it has enough for domestic use before it sells any to India.

(A Closer Look, page 56)

Left: Bangladesh is the world's largest producer of jute. The demand for jute today is low because many of the bags that used to be made of jute are now made of plastic.

Left: Fish and other seafood are plentiful in the waters near Cox's Bazar. Fishing is an important industry in Bangladesh because it makes export of frozen seafood possible.

types of fruits. Rice is an especially important crop because it is a major staple in the Bangladeshi diet. Jute, on the other hand, is predominantly an export crop. Cattle and poultry are reared for meat.

Industry

Much of Bangladesh's industry is an extension of the country's agricultural sector and is devoted to processing crops, such as jute, sugarcane, and tea. The most important industry in Bangladesh, however, is making clothes for export. Bangladesh also produces paper, cement, and fertilizers. About 10 percent of the country's workforce is employed in the industrial sector.

Transportation

Because building bridges over the country's many rivers is an expensive long-term project, the country's waterways themselves are used for transportation. The major waterways provide access between large cities and towns and are even wide enough for cargo ships. Chittagong is home to the country's main seaport, while Dhaka, Barisal, Chalna, Chandpur, and Narayanganj have major river ports.

POLLUTION

Air and water pollution are serious problems in urban Bangladesh. Underregulated industrial operations and vehicles, including buses, cars, and baby taxis, or three-wheeled motorcycles, are among the main causes.
(A Closer Look, page 60)

GARMENT FACTORIES

In recent years, many Bangladeshi women have begun to work in garment factories. Although the wages are low, many women are happy to work in these factories because working outside the home gives them a sense of independence.
(A Closer Look, page 46)

RICKSHAWS

Rickshaws are an inexpensive way to get around in Bangladesh. Bangladeshi rickshaw owners take pride in decorating their rickshaws, which are often brightly colored and adorned with detailed paintings on the side and back panels.
(A Closer Look, page 64)

People and Lifestyle

In 2002, Bangladesh had a population of more than 133 million people. Bangladeshis aged fourteen and younger formed just over one-third of the population, while nearly 63 percent were aged between fifteen and sixty-four. Less than 4 percent of Bangladeshis were aged sixty-five and older. Estimates suggest that Bangladeshi women give birth to an average of between two to three children each in their lifetimes.

According to figures from 1998, the majority of Bangladeshis — 98 percent — are ethnic Bengalis. The remaining 2 percent consists of non-Bengali peoples of various tribal groups.

Different Social Classes

Hindu Bangladeshis, like Hindus elsewhere in the world, are members of social classes called castes. Each caste is governed by specific religious laws that define who the person can have as friends, whom they can marry, and the civil liberties they have. Intermarriage between castes is rare. Muslim Bangladeshis also observe a certain social hierarchy, although its importance has declined considerably in the second half of the twentieth century. Historically, a small group of Muslims, known as *ashraf* (AH-shrahf), were considered upper class because they descended

OVERPOPULATION AND POVERTY

More than two-thirds of Bangladeshis live below the poverty line. Inadequate employment opportunities for a country so intensely overpopulated has caused many families to live under impoverished conditions and often without the most basic of necessities.
(*A Closer Look, page 58*)

HINDU CASTES

Five castes make up Hindu society. From highest to the lowest, the Brahmin, the *kshatriya*, the *vaishya*, the *shudra*, and the untouchables.

TRIBAL PEOPLES

Most of Bangladesh's non-Bengali tribal groups inhabit the Chittagong Hill Tracts. About twelve groups are known to exist in the area. The Chakma, Mro, Tripura, and Marma peoples form the four largest groups. The Marma are also known as Magh or Mogh, and the Tripura are also called the Tipra.
(*A Closer Look, page 70*)

Left: Three Hindu girls pose with their Muslim friend.

Above: A modern Bangladeshi family spends a leisurely afternoon at the beach.

from esteemed Muslim officials from countries such as Turkey, Afghanistan, and Iran. Some members of ashraf can trace their roots back to the Prophet Mohammed. Ordinary Muslims form the larger group called *atraf* (AH-trahf). Increasingly, however, a person's social class in Bangladesh is determined by the amount of land one owns, one's job, or one's level of education.

Extended Family

Called a *poribar* (POH-ree-bahr), the traditional basic family unit in Bangladesh consists of a husband and wife, their unmarried children, and their married sons and their families. A poribar often includes several generations. Unmarried Bangladeshis may live with their parents and extended family consisting of grandparents, uncles and aunts, cousins, nieces, and nephews on their father's side of the family. The poribar is headed by the oldest man in the family, and the eldest woman is also shown much respect. In the countryside, a poribar may occupy three or four houses surrounding a courtyard. Food is shared and chores are divided among the extended family members.

Most urban families live in small houses that are made from either wood or bricks and have tin roofs. Poorer families tend to live in makeshift roadside shacks that are typically made of scraps of wood or cardboard and sheets of tarpaulin. Only wealthy families have solidly built homes.

CLASS AND CLOTHING

Clothing can sometimes indicate a person's social class. A poor man usually wears a *lunghi* (LUNGE), which is a type of sarong, a t-shirt or shirt, and rubber sandals or no footwear at all. A man of higher socioeconomic status may choose to wear a Punjabi suit, which is usually white. White indicates that a person does not perform manual labor and is, therefore, of a higher class. For women, the type of fabric worn and the decoration on the fabric reflect socioeconomic status.

Gender Differences

Bangladeshi society is patriarchal, or male-dominated, in every aspect of life. Most females are submissive to the men in their households, whether it is her father or her husband. Bangladeshi women have few legal rights. If a woman's husband dies, she usually inherits no money or property. Instead, the inheritance is usually divided equally among her sons, whose duty it is to take care of their mother.

Bangladeshi women generally have limited opportunities in education and employment. Traditionally, they tend to be homemakers, while men work outside the home. Today, more and more women, especially in the urban areas, work outside the home. Although two women have served as the country's prime minister, Bangladeshi women are generally not active in politics.

Purdah (PAWR-dah) is the Islamic practice of physically separating men and women after they have reached puberty. Although the degree to which purdah is practiced in Bangladesh varies from region to region, it is common for men and women to be separated in many social situations. Bangladeshi men and women generally do not even shake hands. Some Bangladeshi women wear a black *burkha* (BOHR-kah). The burkha resembles a long gown that covers the entire body, except for the eyes,

MARRIAGE

Marriages in Bangladesh traditionally have been arranged by parents or close relatives of the couple getting married. Modern Bangladeshis, especially those residing in urban areas, are increasingly less likely to abide by this custom. In Islamic culture, it is customary for a man or his family to pay a dowry to his future wife's family, and a Muslim man may have up to four wives. Divorce is allowed under Islamic law but is usually not an option under Hindu customs. Should the need arise, a court of law can arrange for a Hindu couple to separate.

THE WOMEN OF BANGLADESH

Islamic fundamentalism and other conservative aspects of Bangladeshi society combine to deny many women basic civil liberties that are taken for granted in many Western countries.
(A Closer Look, page 72)

Left: Cultural rules and expectations, especially those relating to interaction between men and women, are often relaxed within university campuses in Bangladesh.

Left: **A combination of conservative values and Islamic fundamentalism has led to much gender inequality in Bangladeshi society. Boys generally enjoy many more civil liberties than girls.**

hands, and feet. Because of the country's population density, people, usually those living in urban areas, are often crowded together, whether on the streets or when using public transportation. Because of social restrictions, Bangladeshi women rarely go into public areas by themselves. Bangladeshi men, on the other hand, are freer to move around in crowded areas. Men are not expected to be as watchful of avoiding physical contact with women as women are expected to be with men.

Children

In Bangladesh, nearly every family favors a male baby over a female one. Nevertheless, the birth of a child, regardless of sex, is a joyous event, and a woman usually gives birth in her mother's home. Customarily, a good luck charm is placed around the baby's waist, and the area around the baby's eyes is blackened with either soot or makeup. Black marks are also applied to the sides of the baby's forehead and the sole of the baby's foot. Bangladeshis believe that these practices will keep the newborn safe from evil spirits. Muslim families also sacrifice a goat or sheep when the baby is named. The women of the family share in the task of raising the family's children. Children are taught to always respect and obey the adults in the household.

HEALTH IN BANGLADESH

Many Bangladeshi hospitals are poorly staffed and have very little equipment and medicine. Raising the country's dismal health-care standards is a pressing task faced by the Bangladeshi government.

(A Closer Look, page 50)

Education

The Bangladeshi educational system consists of three main stages — primary, secondary, and higher education. Primary, or elementary, school is free and compulsory for all Bangladeshi children. The law, however, is inadequately enforced, and estimates suggest that only about half of all school-age children attend school. Many school-age children either have to work to help support their families or stay at home to take care of younger brothers and sisters. Primary education lasts for five years.

Secondary school is divided into three stages — junior secondary (three years), secondary (two years), and higher secondary (two years). Secondary school students must complete each stage before they are allowed to proceed to the next. At the end of secondary education, an examination is given, and only students who have passed are issued the certificate that allows them to enter a university. Secondary education is not free, and few families can afford to send their children to secondary school.

Bangladeshi primary and secondary schools teach either in Bangla or in English. Schools that teach in English are usually private, and tuition is costly. Most schools that teach in Bangla are publicly funded, and separate schools are run for boys and girls. Some students choose to be educated in *madrashas* (MAH-drah-shahs), or Islamic religious schools. Madrashas educate

THE HISTORY OF EDUCATION IN BANGLADESH

The Bangladeshi educational system of today can trace its roots back to the time of British rule. Since then, Bangladesh's educational system has undergone several major changes. During British rule, for example, only the wealthy and upper-class members of society were able to receive an education. Bengalis, even those from wealthy families, were considered second-class citizens. When Bangladesh was known as East Pakistan, there was greater opportunity for a local Bengali to obtain an education but still only available to those whose families could afford to send them to school. Although English was the language of instruction at that time, the sociopolitical conditions were such that a person had to speak and write Urdu, the official language of Pakistan, in order to gain employment after graduation. This greatly limited the opportunities of the people from East Bengal.

Left: These children in Sunamganj are attending a rural school. A shortage of teachers and overcrowding in existing schools are problems faced by the Bangladeshi government.

Left: **These rural women are attending an adult literacy class. Bangladesh's literacy rates are among the lowest in South Asia. In 2000, nearly half of Bangladeshis aged fifteen and older were unable to read or write. More men than women are literate in the country.**

very poor children free of charge. Students at madrashas are housed, fed, and taught the Islamic doctrines by religious elders. Such schools are closely linked to mosques and often rely on public donations to fund their operations. A small number of international schools in Bangladesh's major cities offer American, French, and British curricula. Students who graduate from these schools generally head for universities outside of Bangladesh.

Higher Education

Bangladesh has numerous institutions of higher education, including several universities and more than 750 postsecondary colleges. Nondegree courses or vocational training in a wide variety of fields, including law, engineering, arts, agriculture, and home economics, can be sought at specific colleges. Bangladesh has public and private universities, including Dhaka University, Bangladesh University of Engineering and Technology, and North South University, and Jahangirnagar University in the Dhaka area, as well as the Bangladesh Agricultural University at Mymensingh and the Islamic University at Kushtia. Rajshahi University and Chittagong University are among the more established. Bangladeshi university students typically come from wealthier families.

Religion

A vast majority of Bangladeshis — about 83 percent — are Muslim. Hindus make up about 16 percent of the country's population. The remaining 1 percent consists of small numbers of Christians, Buddhists, and followers of animistic beliefs.

Islam was first introduced to the region at the beginning of the 1200s. Although most Bangladeshis today are Muslim, Hinduism was the dominant religion of the region up until the late 1800s. In 1988, Bangladesh's constitution was amended, and Islam was declared the state religion. Although Bangladeshis in general practice a great deal of religious tolerance, respecting beliefs different from their own, some religious tensions remain.

Islam

Muslims throughout the world divide into two main branches — Sunnis and Shi'ites. Most Muslim Bangladeshis are Sunnis. Shi'ites in Bangladesh are mostly descendants of early Iranian immigrants. Although they follow different doctrines, Sunni and

CHRISTIANITY

A small number of Bangladeshis are Christian. Most Christian Bangladeshis are descendants of early Portuguese settlers and have Portuguese surnames, such as Gomes, Dias, and Gonsales. In the 1500s, many Portuguese sailors and traders arrived in India, and some went on to marry local women.

Below: **Built in 1967, the Baitul Mukarram Mosque in Dhaka is filled with worshipers every Friday, the Islamic holy day.**

Left: **Because tensions still exist between Bangladesh's Muslim majority and its Hindu minority, security forces are often present at major Hindu festivals to ensure that mob behavior and social unrest do not arise.**

Shi'ite Muslims actually share many practices, such as abstaining from pork and alcohol and fasting from dawn to dusk during the holy month of Ramadan. Muslims also aim to pray five times a day. In Islamic culture, the weekend spans Friday and Saturday. Friday is regarded as a holy day, and activity centers around the morning prayer session at a mosque. Many government offices and some shops are closed on Fridays.

Every village has at least one small mosque and an *imam* (IH-mahm), or religious elder. A respected figure, the imam lives true to the laws of Islam and is a spiritual leader and inspiration to his community.

Hinduism

Hinduism is the second-largest religion in Bangladesh. At the heart of Hinduism is the belief in reincarnation and also the belief that beef should never be eaten because the cow is a sacred animal. Hindus also recognize many gods and goddesses, such as Krishna, Ram, Kali, Shiva, and Ganesh, whom they worship with rituals and celebrate with festivals. Because the country is heavily agricultural, Hindu Bangladeshis pay special attention to Durga, the goddess of nature. Hinduism's holy men are called Brahman priests. In Bangladesh, Hindus are concentrated in Khulna, Jessore, Dinajpur, Faridpur, and Barisal.

BUDDHISM

Buddhists form a tiny minority in Bangladesh. Buddhism is mainly practiced among the tribal peoples dominating the Chittagong Hill Tracts, including the Chakma, Marma, and Mro peoples. Buddhist temples and monasteries (*below*) are peppered throughout Chittagong and Cox's Bazar, areas that border Myanmar.

Language and Literature

In 1952, when what is now Bangladesh was East Pakistan, conflicts arose between East and West Pakistan because the people of East Pakistan did not want to adopt Urdu as their official language. Today, Bangla, also known as Bengali, is the official language of Bangladesh. Spoken by about 98 percent of the population, Bangla is considered the mother tongue of the land. Although many Bangladeshis speak a little bit of English, the language is most fluently spoken among those who are well-educated. Nearly forty other languages are spoken by minority ethnic groups in Bangladesh. The more common ones include Arakanese, Chakma, Chittagonian, Garo, Sadri, Santali, Sylhetti, and Tippera.

One of the Indo-European languages, Bangla developed partly from Sanskrit and is spoken not only by Bangladeshis but also by ethnic Bengalis elsewhere. Some people in Calcutta, India, for example, speak Bangla. Words from Portuguese, Engish, Arabic, Hindi, and Farsi, have been incorporated into Bangla over time.

Left: Daily Bengali and English newspapers are available in Bangladesh. Apart from Bangladesh Television (BTV), a government-run station, several privately owned companies also provide cable television services that allow access to international news programs and entertainment. Nine government-funded radio stations also operate in the country.

Left: **A well-loved poet and philosopher, Rabindranath Tagore (*left*) traveled widely in his life. He was photographed with Mahatma Gandhi (*right*) in Santiniketan, India, in 1940.**

Oral Tradition

Bangladesh has a rich oral tradition. Traditional Bangladeshi storytellers, who are usually men, can take up to seven hours to tell an epic tale. Storytellers are well-rounded performers who narrate, sing, dance, and mime to tell a story. Bangladeshi stories often tell of princes and princesses and magical figures such as fairies. The storyteller plays all the characters in the story and portrays each of them through actions and by changing the tone of his voice or the expression on his face.

Literature

For several centuries, Bangladeshi literature was characterized by folk ballads and stories. Poet Rabindranath Tagore (1861–1941) is probably the greatest figure in Bengali literature. Tagore played an important role in the revival of Bengali culture in the 1800s and was awarded the Nobel Prize for Literature in 1913. Although Tagore hails from West Bengal, India, Bangladeshis revere him because he helped preserve their language and culture. In fact, Tagore wrote Bangladesh's national anthem and has had some of his poems put to music and made into songs. Another important literary figure in Bangladesh is Kazi Nazrul Islam, a poet and playwright. He has been described as the "rebel poet" and the "voice of nationalism and independence."

PATUAGAN

Patuagan (POH-too-ah-gahn) is the ancient art of storytelling that involves bringing to life a story depicted on a painted scroll. From as far back as 2 B.C., stories were painted on cloth scrolls. Each scroll was divided into a series of panels, and each panel told part of a story. A storyteller would hang the scroll near where he was performing and point to the different panels as he told the story. Musicians or singers sometimes accompany the storyteller. The story of Ghazi is a famous example of a painted-scroll story. A fifteenth-century Muslim general, Ghazi was made a saint because he is said to have performed miracles, one of which was bringing dead trees back to life.

Arts

Traditional Bangladeshi Music

Traditional Bangladeshi music includes both classical and folk music, and each type of music has different performing styles. All forms of Bangladeshi classical music can be performed vocally or instrumentally. They sound different from Western music because they are based on the Indian system of musical tones. Ustad Alauddin Khan and Ustad Ayet Ali Khan are two well-known Bangladeshi classical musicians. The instruments most commonly used in Bangladeshi classical music are Indian in origin and include the tabla and the sitar.

Baul (BAH-ul), marfati (MAH-for-tee), and jari (JAH-ree) are examples of types of Bangladeshi folk music. Bangladeshi folk instruments include the banshi (BAH-shee), which is a flute made of wood or bamboo; the dhole (DHOHL), or wooden drums; the dotara (DOH-tah-rah), a four-stringed instrument; and the mandara (MAHN-dah-rah), or small cymbals.

MODERN MUSIC IN BANGLADESHI

Modern Bangladeshi music is influenced by both Middle Eastern and Western musical styles. The mixture of Western instruments, such as the guitar, saxophone, synthesizer, and drums, with traditional Bangladeshi instruments gives the music a unique feel. Shumana Huq is a famous Bangladeshi pop singer.

Left: **Guests at the Sonargaon Hotel in Dhaka are treated to a performance of Bangladeshi classical music. In such concerts, members of the ensemble usually each play a solo to display their skills on their instruments.**

Bangladesh Dance and Drama

Classical dance in Bangladesh has been heavily influenced by Indian styles and also by folk and tribal dances from Bangladesh itself. Famous Bangladeshi classical dances, such as *kathak* (KOH-thohk) and *bharatnatyam* (BHAH-raht-naht-yah), are similar to those performed in India, while *dhali* (DHAH-lee), *manipuri* (MOH-nee-poo-ree), and snake dances are some of the country's more famous folk dances. The Bulbul Academy and the Nazrul Academy, both in Dhaka, are two schools where Bangladeshi girls can learn Bangladeshi classical dancing.

Theater is a popular art form in Bangladesh, and many Bangladeshi theater groups perform plays written both locally and abroad. The Dhaka Theatre and the Nagarik Nattya Sampraday are two well-known theater groups. In Dhaka, plays are often performed at Dhaka University and the Museum Auditorium. *Jatra* (JAH-trah) is a type of folk drama that acts out traditional myths and folklore. Heroism, love, and tragedy are common themes in traditional jatra, but modern jatra performances have also begun to include social and political commentary. Such plays are usually accompanied by music and dance and are performed mainly in villages, where they most often take place during harvest celebrations or fairs.

Above: Dressed in colorful saris, these graceful dancers are performing a dance about catching fish. Almost all dances in Bangladesh are performed by women, who train for years to perfect special movements of the hands, feet, and head.

TELEVISION SOAP OPERAS

Bangladeshis enjoy television soap operas, which often reflect modern Bangladeshis' views on life, love, and family in modern times. In Dhaka, it is not uncommon to see film crews on the streets shooting scenes for various soap operas.

Architecture

Historical Bangladeshi architecture — ranging from ancient Buddhist and Hindu temples to mosques and European-style churches — reflects the various ruling cultures that influenced the country throughout its long and tumultuous history.

Modern, Western-style architecture gained a strong presence in Bangladesh only in the mid-1900s. Since then, many homes in Dhaka that were built on large, private estates have been replaced by tall apartment buildings in an effort to provide more housing for the country's rapidly growing population. Some of these buildings combine elements of both Western and South Asian architecture, showing creative design and use of color.

Because many people in Bangladesh are so poor, village architecture is evident even in urban areas, including Dhaka. Village houses are usually made from dried mud, bamboo, or brick and have roofs made of thatch or corrugated metal sheets. Because flooding is common in Bangladesh, houses are often built on wooden platforms or stilts. The interior of a village house typically consists of a simple rectangular space, which most

HISTORICAL SITES AND TREASURES

Bangladesh has a rich array of historical sites and architecture that provide a glimpse into the lives and cultures of the country's early inhabitants. The ruins of Paharpur, Bagerhat, and Mahasthangarh are some of the country's more significant historical sites.
(A Closer Look, page 52)

Below: **These newly built village huts dot the lush countryside.**

32

Left: The National Museum of Bangladesh is relatively new. It is located in Dhaka.

HANDICRAFTS

Bangladesh has rich handicraft traditions. Terra-cotta pottery and sculpture are forms of folk art that were first produced in ancient times. Small statues of animals and people, as well as water jugs and other practical items, are molded from terra-cotta clay. Other Bangladeshi handicrafts include metalwork; jewelry made of precious metals such as silver and gold; and basketry. (*A Closer Look, page 48*)

people fill with the little furniture they can afford. Furniture, especially items made of wood, is expensive in Bangladesh. Because of the hot and humid climate, verandas are a common feature of village houses. Kitchens and toilets are usually housed in smaller, separate structures built away from the village houses. Compounds, consisting of several village houses, are usually built around courtyards. Some compounds have access to a nearby river or pond.

Museums

The National Museum was established in 1913. Inside, the museum is divided into a series of smaller galleries, which cover subjects such as natural history, history and classical art, ethography and decorative art, and contemporary art and world civilization. Examples of Bangladeshi fine art and folk art, as well as important mementos of the Liberation War, are exhibited at the National Museum. Other museums in Bangladesh include the Ethnological Museum in Chittagong; the Archaeological Museums at Lalbagh Fort, Mahasthangarh, Paharpur, and Mainamati; and the Tribal Cultural Museum in Rangamati. The Tribal Cultural Institute supervises the Tribal Cultural Museum, which preserves and showcases native costumes and other cultural items from the tribal peoples of Bangladesh.

TRADITIONAL CLOTHES AND TEXTILES

The finely embroidered quilts, called *nakshi kantha* (NOHK-shee KAHN-thah), are unique to the Bengal region of Asia. *Jamdani* (JAHM-dah-nee) is an expensive type of fabric that has been described as "woven air" because of the fabric's sheer, or near see-through, quality. Artistically decorated, the jamdani is often made of muslin or silk and is uniquely Bangladeshi. (*A Closer Look, page 68*)

Leisure and Festivals

Leisure and Recreation

Bangladeshis are a friendly and hospitable people who love to spend time with family, friends, and visitors. Bangladeshis are always polite to their guests and make it a point to offer their guests refreshments, even if it is only a glass of cold water, and a place to sit. In Bangladeshi culture, it is improper for a visitor to sit on the floor or ground. Often, when Bangladeshis meet, they say *Salaam aleykum* (sah-LAAM ah-LIE-koom), which means "Peace be unto you." This greeting originated in Islamic traditions.

Because the country suffers from intense overcrowding, finding a quiet place to relax in Bangladesh's urban centers can be difficult. Some people choose to relax and enjoy themselves on the weekends, which in Bangladesh means Fridays and Saturdays, in the small parks found throughout the country. In the parks, groups of women can be seen strolling together and chatting, while younger Bangladeshis may be playing soccer or

Below: **Children in rural Bangladesh still play many traditional games, such as jumping rope, that have become unpopular in urban areas.**

engaging in more traditional recreational activities such as spinning tops and flying kites. Sometimes, small game stalls are set up in the parks. The most popular of these involves shooting balloons with a rifle. Small groups of people may gather to listen to amateur musicians similar to street musicians in Western countries. Various food vendors also station themselves outside the parks, where they sell treats such as popcorn, spiced nuts or grains, and peeled cucumbers and carrots.

In recent years, several theme parks have been built in Bangladesh, and a favorite family outing is to spend the day at one of these establishments. The admission costs, however, range from affordable to high, which reserves this activity for middle-class to wealthier Bangladeshis. Bangladeshis love for drama means that watching movies, plays, and television are popular forms of entertainment. Concerts featuring traditional or modern music are also well-attended.

In Dhaka, nearly every street corner is marked by a makeshift tea stall. The stall owner sells hot, sweet, milky tea and an assortment of biscuits. Customers of these stalls are usually men, who usually sit on wooden stools and chat with strangers or catch up with friends over their cups of tea. Rickshaw drivers stopping to rest between trips also tend to gather at these tea stalls.

Left: **Bangladeshi batsman Alok Kopali (*left*) swings his bat while Sri Lankan wicketkeeper Prasanna Jayawardena (*center*) and fielder Hashan Thilakaratne (*right*) look on. The two teams were playing their second Test match on July 29, 2003 on the cricket field of the Sinhalese Sports Club in Colombo, India.**

Sports

The Bangladeshi government has shown strong support for the development of sports in the country and favors team sports because they are communal activities. Cricket, soccer, and field hockey are some examples of team sports that Bangadeshis frequently play, whether professionally or as recreation.

Bangladeshis also love a game of badminton or table tennis. Badminton is one of the few sports that many Bangladeshi women play. Badminton courts can be found in nearly every part of Bangladesh, even in rural villages. Wrestling is a sport that interests mostly young men.

Cricket

Many Bangladeshis are big fans of cricket. Throughout the country, informal cricket games can be seen just about everywhere, and matches at the Bangabandhu National Stadium in Dhaka and at smaller stadiums throughout the countryside are always well attended by supporters of both teams. The Bangladeshi national team plays internationally and won regional acclaim at the 1997 International Cricket Council Trophy tournament held in Malaysia. Mohammad Aminul Islam and Akram Khan are famous Bangladeshi cricket players. Bangladesh played its first Test match, the most respected form of cricket competition, in 2000.

BANGLADESH AND TEST CRICKET

International cricket matches are played at many levels, and Test cricket matches are the most prestigious and challenging. Test matches are played only by the world's best national teams, which the International Cricket Council selects by granting the team Test status. The Bangladeshi national team earned its Test status in 2000, but some observers have since called for the privilege to be withdrawn because of the team's poor performance in recent Test matches.

The National Sport of Bangladesh

Kabaddi (KAH-bah-dih) is played by two teams of seven. A game consists of two main parts. In the first part, each team tries to capture as many of the opposing team's members as possible by touching them while running within a marked area. Touching opponents indicates that they have been captured and are, therefore, out of the game. The first part ends when all the members of one team have been captured. The team that won the first part then chooses one member to play the first segment of the second part. The second part begins when the representative from the first-half winners enters the opposing court chanting "kabaddi." This player then tries to touch as many members of the opposing team as possible and return to his side of the court without taking a breath. The first-half losers will try to avoid and distract their pursuer until he has to take another breath. If the player from the first-half winners returns on the same breath, then the players whom he touched, if any, are out of the subsequent segments. If not, then the first-half losers win the first segment of the second half. The teams switch roles in the second segment and continue to alternate roles in subsequent segments until all the members of one team are out of the game.

Left: **Kabaddi is played on a court that measures about 150 square yards (125 square meters) and has been divided into two halves. Each kabaddi team is actually made up of twelve players, but only seven players are active at one time; the remaining five are on reserve.**

Religious Festivals

The main festivals in Bangladesh are religious. Because the Muslim, Hindu, and Buddhist calendars are different from one another and also from the Gregorian calendar, religious holidays in Bangladesh tend to fall on different days each year.

Eid-ul-Fitr is the country's most celebrated Muslim festival. A joyous and festive time, *Eid-ul-Fitr* is celebrated over three days in Bangladesh, during which people receive gifts, wear new clothes, and have family gatherings. *Eid-ul-Azha* is the second most celebrated Muslim festival and marks the time of *hajj* (HAWJ), which is a pilgrimage to Mecca all Muslims try to make at least once in their lives.

Durga Puja, an important Hindu festival, takes place around mid-October and lasts for five days. On the last day of the festival, worshippers gather at their local temples with their colorful clay-and-bamboo representations of the goddess Durga to pray to her. In Dhaka, the Dhakeswari Temple draws the largest number of worshippers, who then make their way to Sadarghat, Dhaka's main river port, near nightfall. There, they place their statues of Durga on temporary floats and then push the statues away from the riverbank so that the statues will eventually sink into the river.

Buddha Purnima is a major Buddhist festival that takes place on the fifteenth day of the fourth lunar month, which usually falls in May. The festival celebrates the birth, enlightenment, and death of Buddha.

Left: A Bangladeshi girl looks at the hundreds of Muslim worshippers praying around her on Eid-ul-Fitr, the most important Muslim festival in Bangladesh. Eid-ul-Fitr marks the end of the Islamic holy month of Ramadan, which is the time during which all Muslims fast from dawn to dusk.

Secular Holidays

Bangladeshis celebrate a series of secular holidays, including *Pawhela Boishakh* (mid-April) and Victory Day (December 16). On Independence Day (March 26), gunshots can be heard throughout Dhaka early in the morning. Later in the day, many Bangladeshis place wreaths at the National Martyrs Monument in Savar. At night, public buildings throughout the country are lit. International Mother Language Day (February 21), which has been endorsed by UNESCO since 1999, was inspired by the people of East Bengal while it was under Pakistani rule. Fiercely protective of their mother tongue, Bangla, the people of East Pakistan firmly resisted the Pakistani government's attempts to make Urdu the official language of the land. Today, celebrations of the holiday in Dhaka begin at the stroke of midnight, when Bangladeshis gather to sing the song "*Amar vaier raktay rangano ekushay February*," which loosely translates into "February 21, the day stained with my brother's blood," to honor those who died defending their mother tongue.

Above: Every year on December 16, Bangladeshis celebrate Victory Day, which marks the end of the Liberation War against Pakistan in 1971.

Food

Bangladeshis typically eat three meals a day. At breakfast, *ruti* (ROO-tee), which is a round, flat bread, is often eaten. Ruti is sometimes served with leftover curries from lunch or dinner the day before. *Pantabhat* (PAHN-tah-bhaht) is a popular breakfast dish and is made by soaking cooked rice in some water overnight so that the rice is slightly fermented by morning. The fermented rice mixture is then eaten with some salt, chilies, and mashed vegetables. Another breakfast dish, *dudh bhat* (DOODH bhaht) is made by mixing cold, leftover rice with either milk or water and *gur* (GURH), or date palm sugar.

In Bangladesh, lunch is the biggest meal of the day. Whether lunch or dinner, Bangladeshi meals typically consist of boiled rice accompanied by one or more curried dishes that may contain vegetables and legumes or a type of meat, such as fish, chicken, lamb, or beef. Combining varying amounts of different spices to form a flavorful seasoning is the basis of Bangladeshi cooking. Recipes for *tarkari* (TAWR-kah-ree), or curries, vary from cook to cook but always combine a great many spices, including cumin, coriander, cloves, and cinnamon.

RICE AND TEA

Rice is such an important part of the Bangladeshi diet that many Bangladeshis could not imagine a day without it. Tea is the country's national drink. The two crops are central to any Bangladeshi's life and have a long history in the country.
(*A Closer Look, page 62*)

FAVORITE DRINKS

Cha (CHAH), or tea, is the national drink. Most Bangladeshis like to drink their tea hot with sugar and milk stirred in. Made from yogurt, *lassi* (LAHS-sih) is another popular beverage. Lassi can be sweet or salty. Roadside stalls throughout the country also commonly sell green coconut juice, which is served directly from the shell of the coconut.

Left: Flat breads such as *parata* (POH-rah-tah) or *naan* (NAHN) are sometimes eaten instead of rice. Parata stalls, such as this one, are found throughout the country. Parata is best eaten when it is hot and crispy and dipped in a spicy curry.

SNACKS

Samosas (sah-MOH-sahs) are a favorite type of snack in Bangladesh. To make samosas, spicy mixtures of various vegetables or meat and vegetables are wrapped in thin pieces of pastry and then deep fried. Other snacks include fried dumplings (*left*), dried chickpeas or peas, and puffed rice. Fruits such as bananas, mangos, lychees, papayas, watermelons, pineapples, coconuts, and jackfruits are also popular snacks.

Korma (KOR-mah) is a rich, mildly spicy curry that involves cooking a type of meat, usually chicken or lamb, in a yogurt-based sauce and ghee. Ghee is a special type of butter that has had the milk solids and water removed from it. Bangladeshi meals are sometimes accompanied by small cups of ghee. People who love robust flavors usually pour the ghee over their rice and mix it in with the rest of their meals. *Daal* (DAAHL), a thick soup made from yellow or orange lentils, tomatoes, and onions and flavored with turmeric, cinnamon, garlic, and cilantro, is a popular dish in the country. *Biryani* (BIH-rih-yah-nih) is a classic rice dish made by cooking a mixture of rice, a type of meat, peas, potatoes, a yogurt sauce, and numerous spices, including cinnamon, saffron, and cardamon, over low heat for prolonged period of time.

Etiquette

Bangladeshis customarily eat with their hands rather than with utensils. Because most Bangladeshis are Muslims, only the right hand is used for eating. The left hand is considered dirty and offensive. When eating, Bangladeshis typically use their fingertips to mix the curry with the boiled rice before gathering the mixture into small portions, which are then placed into the mouth. Bangladeshis wash their hands both before and after meals. A water basin and towels are always provided so that those who have just eaten can clean their hands. Rose petals are sometimes left to soak in the basin to give the water a pleasant scent.

SWEETS

Many sweets in Bangladesh feature either milk or rice as the main ingredient. *Sandesh* (SHOHN-dehsh), for example, is a dessert made from milk, sugar, nuts, and cardamom. Other sweets include *zorda* (JORH-dah), which is made from sweetened cooked rice and nuts, and *mishti doi* (MEESH-tee doy), which is sweetened yogurt. *Rasgolla* (RAWSH-oh-goh-lah) is usually white in color and is made from milk, sugar, and cream of wheat, while *kalajam* (KAH-loh-jahm) is dark brown outside and pink inside and is made from milk, sugar, flour, and ghee. A wide variety of pastries, called *pitha* (PEE-thah), can be either fried, baked, or boiled. Some of these pastries resemble Western cakes and biscuits.

A CLOSER LOOK AT BANGLADESH

Bangladesh may be a young nation, but the history of the land is long and rich. Of the country's many historical sites, the earliest dates back to the third century B.C. The natural environment of Bangladesh is no less intriguing. Because Bangladesh is the meeting point of three major river systems, waterways reach nearly every part of the country. The Sundarbans, one of the world's largest mangrove forests and home of the rare Royal Bengal Tiger, dominate the country's south.

Today, Bangladesh is struggling against a host of social and economic problems, including overpopulation, extreme poverty,

Opposite: **Dhaka's wharf is always bustling with activity. Paddle-wheeler ferries run between Dhaka and the port of Khulna.**

and inadequate health-care facilities. In the urban areas, air and water pollution are serious health hazards because of motor vehicles and factories. Although Bangladesh has an enormous reserve of natural gas, which has the potential to better the country's sluggish economy, the government has yet to exploit it as an export product.

For ordinary Bangladeshis, rice and tea are probably the two most important items in their diets. The tribal peoples of southeastern Bangladesh form a tiny minority of the country's population and lead very different lives.

Above: **Rickshaws can be found everywhere in Dhaka, although they are gradually being confined to smaller roads. Rickshaw rides are inexpensive and an important means of transportation for many Bangladeshis.**

A Country of Rivers

The network of rivers connecting different parts of Bangladesh is among the world's most complicated river systems. More than 5,000 miles (8,045 km) of waterways, including more than 3,000 miles (4,827 km) of cargo routes, flow through Bangladesh before eventually emptying into the Bay of Bengal. Bangladeshis take great pride in the country's plentiful rivers, which group into three main river systems — the Brahmaputra-Jamuna, the Ganges-Padma, and the Meghna. Some rivers in the Chittagong region are independent of the three systems.

River Transportation

As many as sixty kinds of boats, from paddle boats to paddle-wheelers, are used to navigate the waterways of Bangladesh. The Bangladesh Inland Waterway Transport Corporation (BIWTC) organizes public transportation services along most of the country's rivers. Dhaka's main riverfront port, Sadarghat, is located off the Buriganga River and has services that take

AN EXTENSIVE RIVER NETWORK

The Jamuna is the lower course of the larger Brahmaputra river. The Jamuna and Ganges rivers merge in central Bangladesh, forming the stretch of river that is known as the Padma. The Padma and Meghna rivers merge near the city of Chandpur before emptying into the Bay of Bengal.

Below: **These people in northern Bangladesh are using a large boat to get from one side of a river to the other.**

travelers to just about every riverfront in the country. The paddle-wheeler service known as "The Rocket" travels the popular route between Dhaka and Khulna, passing the major ferry crossing Aricha, where the Jamuna and the Padma rivers meet. The journey passes through areas of lush vegetation, and people traveling on the river sometimes see river dolphins.

During the monsoon season, river transportation may become unreliable because of flooding from heavy rains and choppy waters from strong winds. During the dry season, on the other hand, sediment sometimes builds up to a point that makes some waterways impassable. Throughout the year, however, millions of passengers and thousands of tons (tonnes) of cargo are transported through the country's water routes.

The Badhia

Bangladesh has a community of boat-dwelling people known as the *badhia* (BAD-ee-ah) or the *bede* (BEH-deh). The badhia live on houseboats with their families, which usually include two or three children. The badhia make up about half of the people seen on the country's rivers. Many badhia make a living by selling pink pearls, which they harvest from river oysters, and jewelry and herbal medicines that they make. Except during the monsoon seasons, the badhia tend to travel in large groups resembling clans. Modern influences and technology, however, are gradually changing their lifestyles.

THE ANCIENT PORT OF CHITTAGONG

In ancient times, Yemini and Arab traders of Babylon used to trade with countries such as India and China, and Chittagong was one of the ports they used in the process of importing and exporting goods. The word "Chittagong" originated from the Arab word "Shetgang," where "shet" means "delta" and "gang" means "river." The Arab traders thought that Chittagong was the delta of the Ganges. Today, Chittagong is a major international port used for commercial and economic activities.

Garment Factories

Bangladesh is a major exporter of factory-made clothes. Garments such as shirts, pants, and dresses are beautifully made by the expert hands of young factory workers in Bangladesh, where more than one million jobs are directly related to the industry. Many U.S. and European companies are attracted by the low prices of garments made in Bangladesh. Clothes made in Bangladesh are inexpensive because of the low labor costs in the country.

The Factory Workers

Workers in Bangladesh's garment factories are mostly women between the ages of fourteen and twenty-nine. Bangladesh currently has no specific laws ensuring minimum wage, and workers at some garment factories are known to receive as little as U.S. $15 a month. A typical work day in a garment factory lasts between fourteen and sixteen hours. Nevertheless, a job in a garment factory is regarded as a relatively good one in Bangladesh, and factory workers are happy to have their jobs. Twice a day, the streets in Dhaka are filled with crowds of

Left: **In a country where women have few opportunities, garment factories have become a way for many young women to support themselves and their families.**

women going to or returning from work in garment factories. Many of these young women live in rural villages but travel to the city for employment.

Improving Working Conditions

Working conditions vary from factory to factory. A few factory owners are known to provide excellent benefits, such as health care and free lunches. One garment factory outside of Dhaka offers workers subsidized housing plans. Workers have the option of buying modest houses near the factory's premises by paying monthly installments directly deducted from their wages. In other factories, however, conditions can be poor. Typically, the management will assign to each shift of workers a specific number of garments to be sewn, and workers have to complete the assignment even if it means that they work past their usual hours without overtime pay. Many factory operators have also been accused of physical, verbal, and sexual harrassment.

In recent years, a growing number of local and international nongovernmental organizations have begun to act as watchdogs against factory owners who unjustly exploit their workers. Bangladesh's National Garment Workers Federation, one such organization, helps workers campaign for better working conditions, benefits, and salaries. Efforts also have been made to reduce the number of children employed in garment factories.

Handicrafts

Bangladeshi handicrafts are often both practical and decorative. The handicrafts made in different parts of Bangladesh reflect the kinds of raw materials readily available in the regions from which they come. Bangladeshi handicrafts are principally made of terra-cotta, jute, straw, bamboo, and cotton.

Terra-cotta Pottery

Terra-cotta has been described as "burnt clay," and Bangladeshis have a long tradition of molding this material. Terra-cotta pots are often used for carrying and storing liquids and foods, and some are painted in bright colors or decorated with paintings of birds, fish, or flowers. Examples of Bangladeshi terra-cotta pottery include the *shokher hari* (SHOK-her HAH-rih), which is a special kind of pot reserved mainly for weddings and special occasions, and the *shora* (SHAW-rah), a uniquely shaped lid for cooking pots. The shora is convex, meaning that it curves upward from edge to center, and has edges that also turn upward.

Weaving Straw and Bamboo

Bangladeshis also make creative use of straw and bamboo to weave various types of mats and baskets. Because Bangladesh

Left: All kinds of clay pots, including pots for water, storage, and flowers, are made in this factory in Dhaka.

Left: **Bangladeshis have many everyday uses for baskets. These villagers in Sylhet are using baskets to carry their belongings while they cling to the top and back of a minibus.**

has a mostly warm and humid climate, straw mats make ideal, cooling floor coverings on which to sleep or sit. A special type of mat, the *sitalpati* (SHEE-tohl-pah-tih), is made from cane that has been soaked in water before it is woven. The word "sitalpati" literally means "cool mat." Pieces of colored straw are sometimes woven into sitalpati to produce decorative designs. Some examples of sitalpati have elaborate designs, such as images of birds, animals, or flowers, woven into them.

In Bangladesh, baskets are most commonly made of bamboo. Different kinds of bamboo are used to make baskets for different purposes — ranging from shopping baskets to containers fishers use to bring in their catch. One popular basket style is flat and horseshoe shaped. Called *kula* (KUH-lah), it is used to sift the impurities from harvested rice. Baskets are sometimes decorated with colored straws or reed.

THE BOTNI

The *botni* (BOHT-nih) is a prayer mat that is traditionally woven by Bangladeshi women for their husbands and fathers. The Botni is commonly maroon or dark blue in color and may be decorated with a verse from the Qur'an or an image symbolic of the weaver's hometown, such as a representation of the village mosque.

Health in Bangladesh

A combination of natural and man-made situations contribute to the numerous health problems in Bangladesh. Inadequate health-care facilities, insufficient government funding, and overcrowding in many parts of the country are among the leading causes of health problems. Bangladesh's public hospitals are generally poorly funded, ill-equipped, understaffed, and intensely overcrowded. The crowded living conditions of many ordinary Bangladeshis also make it difficult to keep people healthy. Contagious diseases such as smallpox and tuberculosis pass easily from one person to another when they live in close quarters. Many Bangladeshis are also vulnerable to illnesses because they suffer from poor nutrition, live without lack of basic sanitation, and are uneducated about hygienic practices.

The spread of malaria and dengue fever is made worse by natural conditions that occur in Bangladesh each year. Both illnesses are spread by bites from infected mosquitoes, which breed rapidly during the monsoon season when stagnant pools of water collect just about everywhere in the country. The

Opposite: **These mothers in the Chittagong region are waiting to have their children immunized by a foreign aid worker. Immunization programs in the area target a range of diseases, including polio and measles. The infant mortality rate in Bangladesh is very high, and nearly half of all surviving newborns are underweight. Many children suffer from iodine deficiencies, which tend to cause mental disabilities and physical handicaps.**

Left: **These Bangladeshis in Brahmanbaria are attending a health education class.**

monsoon season is also when a number of water-borne diseases, including typhoid, cholera, and dysentery, become dangerously widespread in a country already struggling with an ailing health-care system.

The Fight Against Polio

Polio is a disease that has been contained in most countries since the mid-twentieth century but remained widespread in Bangladesh until the 1990s. The disease is caused by a virus that attacks the nervous system and sometimes leads to death. Survivors are crippled for the rest of their lives. In Bangladesh, poor sanitation and high population density were the major factors that allowed the disease to spread. In 1988, the World Health Assembly started a campaign aimed at freeing the world of polio. Community education and the introduction of a National Immunization Day have since greatly advanced Bangladesh's fight against the disease. By 1999, only twenty-nine cases of polio were reported in the country, and in 2000, Bangladesh had only one known polio sufferer. Although the end seems near, Bangladesh's fight against polio will continue for some time more. The country is still on the list of ten most-at-risk countries issued by the World Health Organization (WHO) but aims to be certified polio-free by 2005.

ICDDRB

International Center for Diarrhoeal Disease Research, Bangladesh (ICDDRB) is a world famous health research institute in Dhaka. ICDDRB attracts researchers from around the world who wish to study diseases common in Bangladesh, such as cholera, dengue fever, tuberculosis, and diarrhetic diseases. Oral Rehydration Therapy (ORT) is one of the most important discoveries to have emerged from ICDDRB. Developed in the later half of the 1960s, ORT is an inexpensive treatment for severe diarrhea and cholera that has saved the lives of more than two million children each year since its discovery.

ORT simply involves drinking a mixture of clean water and some powdered medicine. People need a certain amount of water inside their bodies in order to stay healthy and can die from dehydration. The drink works to restore a healthy fluid balance for people who have lost too much water from their systems, such as those who have been suffering from severe diarrhea or cholera, which leads to severe diarrhea.

Historical Sites and Treasures

Mahasthangarh

Bangladesh's oldest archaeological site, Mahasthangarh dates back to the third century B.C. and is a magnificent historical landmark. Located on the western bank of the Karatoa River and just 11 miles (18 km) away from the town of Bogra, Mahasthangarh is sacred to Hindus, who gather there once every twelve years in mid-April to take part in a religious bathing ceremony. A museum at Mahasthangarh preserves and exhibits various items recovered from the site, including terra-cotta pieces, gold ornaments, and coins.

Paharpur

Located about 47 miles (75 km) from the city of Bogra, the ruins at Paharpur are famous as part of the "largest monastery south of the Himalayas." Dating back to about the seventh century, the monastery had a total of 177 rooms, which were protected by

LALBAGH FORT

Located in old Dhaka, the Aurangabad Fort is better known as the Lalbagh Fort (*below*). The estate covers an area of 865,600 square feet (80,414 square meters) and within it are numerous historic structures and features. The more significant of which are the three-domed mosque, a bathhouse, and a beautiful garden.

walls measuring between 12 and 15 feet (3.6 and 4.6 m) tall and 16 feet (5 m) thick. Established in the 1950s, the onsite museum showcases a collection of objects recovered from the ruins. The Varendra Research Museum at Rajshahi also holds a number of items recovered from the monastery.

Above: **The lush greenery surrounding the Shait Gumbaj Mosque in Bagerhat gives it an added sense of serenity.**

Bagerhat

The town of Bagerhat was declared a World Heritage Site by UNESCO in 1985. Located near the intersection of the Ganges and Brahmaputra rivers, Bagerhat is famous for the number of historical monuments in the region. The Shait Gumbaj Mosque, the Mazhar Khan Jahan Ali, and the Khodla Math Temple are among the more important.

Built in 1459, the Shait Gumbaj Mosque is the largest and grandest of the traditional mosques in Bangladesh. The name "Shait Gumbaj" translates into the "mosque with sixty domes." The mosque, in fact, has seventy-seven domes, which are supported by sixty stone columns. The building's robust brick exterior is dark with age, and its walls are about 7 feet (2 m) thick.

An Influential Leader

Sheikh Mujibur Rahman (1920–1975) is revered by many Bangladeshis today as Bangabandhu, or the "Friend of the Nation." A prominent speaker during the independence movement that led to the 1971 war of liberation against Pakistan, Sheikh Mujib believed that the political, cultural, and religious differences between the people of East and West Pakistan were sufficient reasons for the creation of an independent Bangladesh.

The Early Years of Independence

Under Mujib, a constitution modeled on the Indian constitution was adopted on November 4, 1972. The first Bangladeshi constitution promised that government in Bangladesh would be guided by four principles — nationalism, socialism, secularism, and democracy. Taken together, these four principles became known in Bangladesh as "Mujibism" or "Mujibbad."

Below: **Sheikh Mujib returned to Bangladesh on January 10, 1972, after being held in West Pakistan as a political prisoner. Although Sheikh Mujib was named the first president of Bangladesh while in exile, he resigned from the position two days after his return and chose, instead, to become Bangladesh's prime minister.**

Left: **Despite his many failed policies, one of Sheikh Mujib's achievements was that he helped Bangladesh become internationally recognized very soon after independence. Bangladesh joined the United Nations on September 24, 1974.**

The Decline of Sheikh Mujib's Rule

Up until the 1973 elections, Sheikh Mujib's leadership, although challenged by corruption and rural lawlessness, was overwhelmingly supported by the people. By 1975, however, the country's economy had plunged to new depths of hardship and suffering, social order decreased, and the people grew disenchanted. That same year, Sheikh Mujib overturned the democratic ideals he had advocated in earlier years in order to maintain his power and position as head of state. He dissolved the country's constitution and created a virtual dictatorship by declaring Bangladesh a one-party state.

Although Sheikh Mujib's calls to increase agricultural and industrial production, end corruption, and fight illegal smuggling were met with enthusiasm from the Bangladeshi people, his economic policies proved to be stumbling blocks rather than stepping stones. By nationalizing Bangladesh's manufacturing and trading institutions, Sheikh Mujib discouraged the development of healthy competition and a vibrant business environment in the country. In addition, outlawing English in education and government and replacing it with Bangla prevented Bangladesh from communicating and trading freely with the rest of the world.

A FAMILY IS ASSASSINATED

Sheikh Mujib's hard-line approach in ruling and reforming Bangladesh created more and more political enemies over time. On August 15, 1975, a group of young army officers carried out a violent coup in which Sheikh Mujib and twelve other members of his family were killed.

Natural Gas

Bangladesh has small reserves of oil but is speculated to possess enormous reserves of natural gas. In 2000, the country was estimated to have about 11 trillion cubic feet (311 billion cubic meters) of natural gas distributed among twenty operating gas fields. Most of the country's major gas fields, such as those in Bibiyani and Habiganj, are located in north- and southeastern Bangladesh, with a few offshore. Located in the Sylhet division, the country's first gas field was discovered in 1955 but commercial production from the field did not begin until the early 1960s.

Rising Domestic Consumption

Nearly 90 percent of Bangladesh's electricity is generated from natural gas. The country's electricity-producing sector and chemical fertilizer industry respectively consume 48 and 23 percent of the country's natural gas output. Other industries, commercial activities, and domestic use account for the use of the remaining 29 percent. As more and more Bangladeshis gain access to electricity, estimates suggest that Bangladesh will need about 6 percent more gas each year for at least the next twenty years to meet the needs of its own population. From 2000 to 2001, Bangladesh produced 373 million cubic feet (10.6 million cubic m) of natural gas.

NATURAL GAS

Natural gas is one of the main sources of energy that people around the world use every day. Natural gas is a nonrenewable resource, which means that it cannot be replenished once used. Similar to crude oil, natural gas takes thousands or, possibly, millions of years to form.

Left: In March 2000, the managing director of Shell Bangladesh, Andrew Vaughan, gave a presentation showing the areas in Bangladesh Shell intended to explore for gas. By August 2003, Shell announced its decision to withdraw from Bangladesh because of the government's sustained refusal to export natural gas.

BNGPP

The Bangladesh Natural Gas Pipeline Project (BNGPP) is an ambitious, multimillion dollar project proposed by U.S.-based Unocal Corporation in November 2001. The pipeline would link Bangladesh and India in order to provide India with direct access to gas exports from Bangladesh. The initial design for the pipeline was that it would be 30 inches (76 centimeters) wide and 847 miles (1,363 km) long, spanning northeastern Bangladesh and central western India, with a lengthy detour through Delhi. The pipeline would have the capacity to move 500 million cubic feet (14 million cubic m) of gas a day.

Unocal wants to build the pipeline spanning the interior of the country. The company plans to sell Bangladesh's natural gas at the India-Bangladesh border to Indian companies. Up until late 2003, the Bangladeshi government has remained hesitant about the proposal. In 1999, when visiting U.S. president Bill Clinton spoke with then Prime Minister Sheikh Hasina about exporting Bangladesh's natural gas, Sheikh Hasina maintained that she would only consider the project if Bangladesh had enough gas to support itself for the next fifty years. In 2001, Sheikh Hasina lost an election to Khaleda Zia, who has since shown greater interest in exporting the country's natural gas but has met with much disapproval from opposition parties and resistance from the Bangladeshi people.

IMPROVING RELATIONS WITH INDIA

India is anxious to build a direct pipeline to Bangladesh for supplies of natural gas, but relations between India and Bangladesh have soured in the past over such issues as border disputes and the treatment of major rivers. Some analysts have suggested that the exercise of exporting natural gas to India could become a bridge for the two nations to mend their differences.

Overpopulation and Poverty

Bangladesh is the world's eighth most populated country and one of the poorest. Although China has the world's largest population and India the second-largest, Bangladesh is three times more populated than India and seven times more populated than China when measured by the number of persons for each square mile (square km) of the country. Despite the success of various family-planning programs, Bangladesh's population is expected to double in between thirty-five to forty years.

The Bangladeshi government has faced great difficulty in providing health care, food, and housing for the population. More than two-thirds of the population lives below the poverty line. Because many Bangladeshis are very poor, malnutrition is a serious problem in the country. Poverty and a shortage of housing have also led many Bangladeshi families to squeeze into uncomfortably small living spaces, in which diseases easily can be transmitted. Poor sanitation facilities and contaminated water sources make contagious diseases common in the country.

FOREIGN AID

Many countries sponsor development programs in Bangladesh. The programs are usually aimed at educating Bangladeshis about more efficient farming methods; promoting the country's export products, such as jute; and developing women's cooperatives, which help housebound Bangladeshi women earn some money through tasks that they can do at home. Some missionary groups also run hospitals and schools that care for impoverished Bangladeshis free of charge. Foreign aid agencies and nongovernmental organizations (NGOs), such as the Red Cross, Save the Children, Habitat for Humanity, and OXFAM, have also actively contributed in Bangladesh.

Left: An aerial view of tightly packed shanties, or makeshift houses, in Dhaka shows the extent of poverty and overcrowding in the capital city.

Above: **In Dhaka, where space is scarce, examples of extreme poverty and relative affluence are often separated by a narrow waterway.**

Fighting Poverty

Founded in 1972 by Fazle Hasan Abed, the Bangladesh Rural Advancement Committee (BRAC) is a Bangladeshi nongovernmental organization. Over the years, BRAC has grown into a large organization with the aim of reducing poverty in Bangladesh by fighting illiteracy and illnesses. BRAC is represented not only in villages but also in cities.

The Grameen Bank was founded in Bangladesh in the 1970s by Muhammad Yunus. His aim was to give small loans of money to very poor people so that they could start their own businesses and gradually become self-sufficient. The majority of the bank's loans are given to women. Among the small businesses that have been started with the help of loans from the Grameen Bank are tailoring and photo-processing shops, providers of telephone services, and livestock-rearing and food-processing facilities. Today, more than one hundred banks in over thirty countries utilize the "micro-lending" that Yunus created, and the lives of many have improved tremendously as a result of his ingenuity, compassion, and efforts.

Pollution

Air Pollution

Dhaka's air quality is among the worst in the world, and it causes thousands of people to become ill each year. Motor vehicles — including buses, cars, and trucks — contribute the bulk of the city's airborne pollutants. Because many of these vehicles are old and poorly maintained, they emit more pollutants than properly serviced vehicles. The number of vehicles has also nearly doubled since 1985. Daily traffic jams, for which Dhaka is notorious, surround the people in and around them with gray smoke that contains high concentrations of carbon monoxide and nitric oxide.

In 2000, the World Bank approved a loan of U.S. $4.7 million to develop the Bangladesh Air Quality Management Project. The project aims to improve Dhaka's air quality through educating mechanics and vehicle owners on how to maintain engines in a way that would produce less harmful exhaust fumes. In late 2002,

Left: Intense traffic jams, such as this one, are a daily occurrence in Dhaka and trap commuters on the roads for hours.

ADDRESSING THE PROBLEM OF ARSENIC

Because experts have concluded that the distribution pattern of arsenic in the country is unpredictable and unrelated to industry, the task of saving Bangladeshis from arsenic poisoning is immensely difficult. With the help of foreign aid agencies, the Bangladeshi government has been working hard to educate the people on how to test their water for arsenic and other harmful chemicals. Other efforts to fight the arsenic problem include conducting regular tests on existing wells (*left*), drilling deeper tube wells, and finding easy and effective ways to purify water that contains arsenic so that it can be made safe to drink.

the Bangladeshi government banned the three-wheeled motorcycles known locally as "baby taxis" from operating on the country's roads. Since then, baby taxis have been replaced with three-wheeled scooters that run on natural gas instead of gasoline or diesel fuel. The United Nations (U.N.) and the Bangladeshi government are also working together to address the problem of air pollution.

Water Pollution

Many Bangladeshis hand-pump their daily water from tube wells. In the early 1970s, international aid agencies, such as the United Nations Children's Fund (UNICEF), sponsored the drilling of several million such wells in the country. The nationwide project was spurred by the growing number of Bangladeshis contracting diseases such as cholera and typhoid through water sources that were contaminated with human waste. At that time, tube wells seemed like the perfect solution to the problem because water drawn from beneath Earth's surface was uncontaminated, and tube wells were relatively inexpensive to create. Years later, however, it was discovered that as many as half of the tube wells in some districts contained arsenic, a chemical that becomes deadly when consumed in large amounts. Prolonged consumption of arsenic in small doses can cause skin cancer, stomach pain, nausea, vomiting, diarrhea, and numb hands and feet.

Rice and Tea

Rice

Rice is used in many ways in Bangladeshi life. An important food crop, rice is almost certainly served at every meal, whether in a main dish, side dish, or dessert. In the Chittagong Hill Tracts, where most of the population is non-Muslim, rice is used to make alcohol. Many Bangladeshis believe that upset stomachs can be relieved by drinking rice water, which is made by boiling some rice in a lot of water until the water turns cloudy white.

Bangladeshis also use rice to make *alpana* (AHL-poh-nah). Alpana is a form of painting mostly practiced by Bangladeshi women who wish to decorate their homes during festivals or for special occasions. Rice powder is mixed with water to form a paste that is used as the finger paint with which women paint on the walls and floors of their homes. Various materials, including spices, stones, and chalk, are sometimes crushed and added to the rice paste to give it color. Turmeric, for example, creates yellow,

Below: The history of rice dates back to before 5000 B.C. in China. Bangladesh has a hot and humid climate, which is ideal for rice cultivation. In 2001, Bangladesh produced nearly 43,000 tons (39,000 tonnes) of rice. China, Thailand, India, and Indonesia were the only countries that produced more rice during that year.

Left: Tea leaves in Bangladesh are picked from early March to early December.

while stones can make gray or brown. Alpana paintings are usually seen at the entrances of homes, in temple courtyards, or before statues of Hindu or Buddhist gods and goddesses. It is widely believed that alpana paintings have powers to protect people from harm.

Tea

In 1857, the British government set up the Malnicherra Tea Estates, the first tea plantations in the territory of present-day Bangladesh. By the beginning of the twentieth century, more than 150 tea estates had been established, and nearly all of them were owned by the British. Today, most tea plantations are owned by wealthy Bangladeshis, although many continue to be run by the British. Most tea plantations in Bangladesh are located in the Sylhet region.

Most of the tea grown in Bangladesh is black tea, and it is rarely sold on its own. The black tea harvested in Bangladesh is usually first shipped to Europe, where it is processed and mixed with other teas, and then sold in Russia, countries in eastern Europe, and countries in the Middle East.

During the early days of tea cultivation in Bangladesh, most of the laborers on the tea estates were from India. Today, a majority of the tea workers are descendants of the original Indian workers. Small Hindu shrines can still be seen on most tea plantations.

TEA PLANTATION WORKERS' UNION

Workers on Bangladeshi tea plantations today are supported by one of the few trade unions in the country. The union helps them achieve better working conditions and benefits. Among the improvements are elementary schools and doctors on site to provide health-care services for the workers and their families and education for their children.

Rickshaws

A rickshaw is a large tricycle with a carriage consisting of a small bench seat, a retractable hood, and a footrest mounted on top of the two back wheels. When the hood is raised, the passenger is protected from the hot afternoon sun or light rain. Rickshaw drivers also carry large plastic sheets with them in case of heavy downpours, during which the plastic sheets are opened up and wrapped around the passengers' legs and feet to keep them dry.

Riding in a rickshaw is a popular, efficient, and inexpensive way to travel short distances in Bangladesh. A ride costs between five and twenty taka, the currency of Bangladesh, or between U.S. $.08 and .35. Locals call a rickshaw driver a *rickshaw wallah* (RIK-shah WAH-lah). To hail a rickshaw by the roadside in Bangladesh, people raise an arm, wave it, and shout, "Hey, *khali* (KHAH-lee)," which literally means "empty." Occasionally, two or three rickshaw drivers may compete with one another over the same customer and vigorously ring their bicycle bells as they race toward the potential passenger. The rider who reaches the customer first wins the customer's business.

THE FIRST RICKSHAW

The first rickshaw was introduced to Dhaka in 1938. It arrived on a steamboat from Calcutta, India. Since then, the rickshaw has become a permanent feature of Bangladeshi life. Today, rickshaws in Bangladesh are made in special shops. A Bangladeshi rickshaw shop is called a *rickshaw mysteri dokan* (RIK-shah MEES-tree DOH-kahn).

Left: **Although two people can comfortably fit on to the bench seat of a rickshaw, some drivers have taken as many as four passengers at once — three people squeezed onto the bench seat and a fourth person sitting perched on the seat's backrest.**

RICKSHAW ART

Decorating rickshaws is a serious art form in Bangladesh. Rickshaw owners take pride in heavily decorating their vehicles. Their detailed efforts individualize their rickshaws. The back and side panels of a rickshaw are typically covered with hand-painted decorations (*left*). The footrest is typically painted either red or blue and decorated with large tacks. The standard blue hood is often trimmed with gold appliqués of different designs. Colorful plastic streamers hang from the seat, and small, metal vases holding plastic flowers are attached to the handlebars. On some rickshaws, short metal chains with hearts or other charms attached to the ends hang from the back.

Because rickshaws are plentiful, Bangladeshis use them for a wide variety of purposes. Aside from use by people who simply seek to go from one place to another, shopkeepers also have been known to transport their goods by rickshaw. Sometimes, the seat is removed so that large bags of grain or wood can fit in the small carriage space. The passenger must then climb up and sit on top of the bags for the length of the journey. Transporting even heavy and bulky objects, such as television sets and large pieces of furniture, has posed no obstacle to gritty and ingenious Bangladeshi rickshaw drivers.

THE BICYCLE MARKET

The bicycle market in the old part of Dhaka has shops that specialize in rickshaw art. Artists paint directly onto the back and side panels of rickshaws. The Taj Mahal, lions wearing business suits, rats serving tea, and village sunsets are among the images that have been seen on Bangladeshi rickshaws.

The Sundarbans

Covering an area of about 540 square miles (1,400 square km), the Bangladesh Sundarbans are a vast forest that was previously considered part of the forest that stretches past the Indian border into the state of West Bengal. The name "Sundarbans" is widely believed to mean "beautiful forest." Located in Khulna in southeastern Bangladesh, the Sundarbans feature many waterways running through mangrove forests, and they contain the point at which the Brahmaputra, Meghna, and Ganges rivers meet before flowing into the Bay of Bengal. UNESCO declared the Bangladesh Sundarbans a World Heritage Site in 1997.

Wildlife and Vegetation

The Bangladesh Sundarbans have more than 1,000 species of animals and plants, including more than 300 Royal Bengal tigers. Other animals that populate the mangrove forest include turtles, porpoises, freshwater dolphins, and spotted deer. More than 300 species of birds, including brown-winged kingfishers, Pallas' sea-eagles, and magpie robins, have also been identified in the Sundarbans. The magpie robin is Bangladesh's national bird.

EARLY INHABITANTS

The first recorded mention of the Sundarbans was in the thirteenth century when Hindu settlers who were fleeing from Muslims hid in the forests. They settled in the area and built many Hindu temples, and they were later joined by the Khiljis who were escaping from the Afghans. During the seventeenth century, factors such as poor climate and the lack of drinking water are believed to have forced these settlers to leave the Sundarbans.

Left: **The Royal Bengal Tiger (***Panthera tigris tigris***), can grow up to 9 feet (2.7 m) in length. This strong and majestic beast can live up to fifteen years in the wild and twenty years in captivity. Usually a night hunter, its diet consists mainly of wild boars, deer, and fish. Until it is too old to hunt for animals, the Royal Bengal tiger is not known to attack human beings. The Sundarbans are the only mangrove forest in the world in which tigers live.**

The forest has beautiful trees and great reserves of fish, providing a rich source of income for its human inhabitants. As much as 45 percent of government-owned timber production comes from the Sundarbans, and 120 species of fish are caught in the forest's waters by commercial fishermen. Reptiles, such as the Estuarine crocodile and the Indian python, are also part of the fauna in the Sundarbans.

Threats to the "Beautiful Forest"

The Sundarbans are a natural barrier to disasters such as cyclones and floods. Together with the Sundarbans National Park in India just across the border from Khulna, the Bangladesh Sundarbans was declared a "reserved forest" in 1878 under the Indian Forest Act. This meant that people could not remove anything from the forest, plant crops there, or construct new buildings in it. The Bangladesh Wildlife Act has protected the wildlife in the Sundarbans from threats such as vegetation damage, hunting, and the setting of fires since 1974. Environmental problems, such as drastic weather changes that destroy the forest along the seaface and pollution from oil and chemical spills, however, continue to plague the Sundarbans and its diverse fauna and flora.

THE JOBS OF THE FOREST

The mangrove forest has many important functions in the environment, aside from providing a natural habitat for plants and animals. Trees that grow in mangrove forests act as a shield against tidal waves that hit the coast. In Bangladesh, where the landscape is largely made up of flat plains, the Sundarbans can protect parts of the inland from devastating floods. In addition, the mangrove forest is also a natural filter that prevents salt water from entering the inland tributaries.

Traditional Clothes and Textiles

Bangladesh produces unique and beautiful fabrics that are made into traditional clothes, as well as household items such as pillowcases, bedspreads, and tablecloths.

Traditional Clothes

Traditional outfits for most Bangladeshi men consist of combining a lunghi with a western-style shirt or t-shirt. A lunghi is usually printed with a checked or batik design. Some Bangladeshi men, usually those who are more affluent, wear Punjabi suits. Punjabi suits for men are usually made of white cotton and consist of loose-fitting pants and a collarless shirt with long shirttails.

Many Bangladeshi women favor brightly colored clothes. The *shalwar kameez* (SAH-loh-ahr kah-MEEZ), which consists of a long, loose-fitting top and matching baggy pants, is one type of outfit Bangladeshi women wear. The top extends past the wearer's knees and resembles a tunic, or gownlike dress. The *dupata* (doh-PAH-tah) is a large shawl that is often draped over a tunic top. Some women use a dupata to cover their heads and faces. The sari is a traditional dress that women wear. A sari

INDIGO

More than 300 fruits, flowers, roots, and other natural materials are used to make a wide range of fabric dyes in Bangladesh. Indigo, which can dye cotton or woolen fabrics a blue or green color, is one of the most widely used. During the rule of the British Empire, the East India Company considered indigo one of its most profitable imports. In the late 1990s, the cultivation and production of indigo dyes experienced a revival in Bangladesh because of Nilkomol (Blue Lotus). The goal of this project was to create employment for underprivileged women in Bangladesh. The project mainly focused on helping the indigenous Garo communities in Mymensingh. It has been very successful and has helped to provide sustainable employment for many village women.

Left: **Fabric shops in Dhaka are typically well stocked with a wide range of materials that women can use to make saris or other traditional clothes.**

consists of a tight-fitting top that reveals part of the torso and a piece of cloth about 18 feet (5.5 m) long. To put on a sari, a woman wraps the cloth around herself, first forming a pleated skirt that reaches her ankles and then using the remaining fabric to cover the front of her body by extending the fabric diagonally from her waist to over her shoulder. The excess cloth at the end of the sari covers the back. Sometimes, the end of a sari is long enough to be used as a headscarf.

Nakshi Kantha

Nakshi kantha are the finely embroidered quilts that are a traditional form of Bengali needlework. Dating back hundreds of years, this art form began with women who recycled their old saris by making them into quilts. The quilts were decorated with traditional motifs or selections of animal designs and symbols, such as the sun, stars, and trees, that come together to represent a story. Nakshi kantha characteristically consist of multiple layers of cloth that are held together by a sewing technique called running stitches. Running stitches usually form one line, which makes them useful for outlining an image or detailing an embroidered design. The top- and bottommost layers of the quilt are always thin and either lightly colored or white so that the embroidery underneath is visible. The finished product is often a personal statement by the woman who stitched it.

IN STORES TODAY

Among the nakshi kantha sold in shops throughout Bangladesh today, the most common design has a *padma* (POD-mah), or lotus, in the center, and a *mandap* (MAWN-dohp), or a tree of life, in each corner. Apart from on quilts, the kantha style of embroidery is also applied to saris and other household items, such as pillowcases, bedspreads, and tablecloths.

Tribal Peoples

The Chittagong Hill Tracts in southeastern Bangladesh are geographically unique in the country. The landscape there consists of open spaces dotted with valleys and hills, sharply contrasting the densely populated flatlands characteristic of the rest of Bangladesh. Most of the people inhabiting the region are also different from the majority of Bangladeshis. They are neither ethnic Bengalis nor Muslims, instead belonging to one of several tribes. Bangladesh's tribal peoples are mostly Buddhist, while others are known to be Hindu, Christian, or animist.

TRIBAL PEOPLES ELSEWHERE

Apart from living in the Chittagong Hill Tracts, tribal groups, such as the Santals, the Khasis, the Garo, and the Hajang, also inhabit areas in northwestern and northeastern Bangladesh.

Twelve Tribes

The Chittagong Hill Tracts are home to twelve main tribes, and these groups are distinct from the lowland-dwelling Bangladeshis in just about every way — appearance, language, way of life, customs, and beliefs. Bangladesh's tribal peoples are known collectively as *jumma* (JOO-mah). The largest tribe, Chakma, makes up about half of the population in the highlands. The Marma and Tripura peoples combine to make up another third. Among the smaller tribes are the Mro, Tengchangya, Khumi, Lushai, Pankhu, Sak, Bowm, Kuki, and Reang peoples. The Mro are believed to be the oldest tribe in the area.

Left: The economy of Bangladesh's tribal peoples is heavily based on agriculture. The tribal peoples are generally poor.

Left: **A member of the Marma tribe, this man is preparing bamboo strips for the building of more huts.**

Disenchantment

When present-day Bangladeshi territory was under British colonial rule, the members of country's highland tribes were the only people who maintained control over their own land. When British rule ended, ethnic Bengali settlers began to enter the Hill Tracts, causing much unhappiness among the indigenous peoples, who were fiercely protective of their territories and cultures. In 1960, the Pakistanis built the Kaptai Lake as part of a project to generate hydroelectricity. The project disrupted the lives of about 200,000 indigenous people in Bangladesh. Some lost their homes, while many others were forced to seek refuge in the nearby Indian states of Assam and Tripura. In the 1970s, waves of ethnic Bengalis, with the support of the government, settled in the Chittagong Hill Tracts. Many of the indigenous people who were displaced from their own lands formed a resistance movement. More than twenty years of violence between government forces and tribal fighters followed. Both sides signed a peace agreement in 1997, but since 2001, tensions have again heightened because the Bangladeshi government, now led by the Bangladesh National Party (BNP) instead of the Awami League (AL), has proposed revising the terms of the peace agreement so that less compensation is owed to the indigenous people of the Hill Tracts.

Below: **This woman is from the Tripura tribe. In 1947, over 90 percent of the population in the Chittagong Hill Tracts were indigenous. By 1991, the Chittagong Hill Tracts had a population of more than 974,000 people, but only about half were jumma. The rest were ethnic Bengalis.**

The Women of Bangladesh

Women in Bangladesh have long suffered a denial of various civil liberties. Although the situation has seen significant improvement in recent years, the struggle for rights and opportunities equal to those of men is far from over.

Women in Politics

Since independence, Bangladesh has held three elections that resulted in a woman becoming prime minister. Begum Khaleda Zia was elected in 1991 and 2001, and Sheikh Hasina Wajed was elected in 1996. Bangladeshi law once reserved thirty seats in parliament for women, but that law expired in May 2001. The Bangladeshi government was proud to have encouraged women's participation in parliament, but some critics have argued that the gesture was superficial because few women served elsewhere in government.

Women in the Arts

In Bangladesh, many cultural barriers remain for women who seek to produce works of art and literature. Culturally, it is

Left: **On International Women's Day (March 8) in 2002, about 200 survivors of acid burns joined nearly 2,000 activists in the streets of Dhaka to call for greater protection for women.**

Left: **In July 1999, six survivors of acid attacks (*back row*) returned to Bangladesh after having received cosmetic surgery in Madrid. The surgeries were performed in a joint effort between Bangladeshi and Spanish doctors.**

preferred that women be the subject of artists rather than the artists themselves. A few female writers and artists, however, have found creative ways to express themselves. Some of them express their disapproval of how various tenets of Islam have been narrowly interpreted to justify the devaluation and restriction of women in Bangladeshi society. Award-winning author Taslima Nasrin is one such figure, and her works have angered many Muslim fundamentalists because they deal with the persecution of Muslim women. Her book *Lajja*, in which she advocated treating men and women as equals, caused such an uproar that the Bangladeshi government banned it. Nasrin has been living in exile since 1994, spending time in the United States, Sweden, and Germany. Today, she lives in France.

Acid Burnings

Some women in Bangladesh have had concentrated sulfuric acid thrown in their faces with the intention of disfiguring them. Revenge is the most common motive for these cruel attacks. A woman who rejects a suitor's advances, for example, may later suffer an acid attack. Bangladesh's Acid Survivors Foundation works to foster support among survivors of acid attacks and also to develop preventive measures through community education. Activist and leader of Naripokho, a human-rights organization, Nasreen Huq works with local police to monitor the problem of acid burnings. Her efforts have gained international support.

WOMEN ARTISTS

Artist and sculptor Novera Ahmed first became famous in the 1950s. Years later, she designed the *Shahid Minar*, a work that commemorates the lives lost in Bangladesh's 1971 Liberation War. Another female artist from Bangladesh is painter Farida Zaman, who has had her paintings exhibited in Asia, South America, and Europe. Zaman enjoys greater recognition internationally than at home.

RELATIONS WITH NORTH AMERICA

Relations between Bangladesh and the United States began on a rocky note and remained uneasy for some years following Bangladesh's official independence in 1972. In 1971, when Bangladesh was fighting its war for independence against Pakistan, the United States supported Pakistan with both military personnel and equipment. As a result, the Awami League, the ruling political party in East Pakistan at that time, continued to view the United States as a threat after the nation of Bangladesh formed. For most of the 1970s, tensions persisted between the two countries even though the United States had formally recognized

Opposite: **A boy holding a basket on his head walks past a poster of former U.S. president Bill Clinton. The poster was part of the effort to welcome Clinton, who made the first visit to Bangladesh by a U.S. president in March 2000.**

newly independent Bangladesh. Anti-U.S. sentiment among Bangladeshis was strong and sometimes led to violent demonstrations, such as the burning of the U.S. Information Service library in Rajshahi in December 1972. By 1978, Bangladesh had become closely aligned with U.S. foreign policy relating to both the Chinese-Vietnamese border conflict and the unrest in Cambodia and Afghanistan. In 1979, the two nations signed the Treaty on the Non-Proliferation of Nuclear Weapons, and the United States set up a nuclear research facility near Dhaka. Today, Bangladesh and the United States share a robust friendship.

Above: **In April 1998, Bangladeshi prime minister Sheikh Hasina Wajed (*left*) and U.S. Army chief of staff General Dennis J. Reimer (*right*) met for talks at Sheikh Hasina's residence in Dhaka.**

Current Relations

Despite the rocky start, U.S.-Bangladesh relations improved tremendously throughout the 1980s and 1990s. Numerous official visits paid by Bangladeshi leaders to Washington, D.C., over the years helped ease the negative effects of U.S. support for Pakistan during the Bangladeshi war for independence. President Zia visited the United States in August 1980; President Ershad visited in 1983, 1988, and 1990; and Prime Minister Khaleda Zia visited in 1992. U.S. foreign policy toward Bangladesh during these years focused on helping the country develop a democratic government and build a stable economy.

Since their reconciliation, the two nations have shown strong support for each other, with Bangladesh lending military support to many U.S.-led causes in recent years. In 1991, Bangladeshi troops were sent to fight in the Persian Gulf War, and in 1994, they joined the multinational military presence in Haiti. Bangladesh has also sent army personnel to serve alongside U.S. forces in various United Nations (U.N.) peacekeeping missions, most recently in Bosnia and Afghanistan.

Below: **In January 2003, the Bangladeshi unit of the U.N. Iraq-Kuwait Observation Mission trained at Camp Khor near the Iraq-Kuwait border.**

Left: **On March 20, 2000, U.S. president Bill Clinton arrived in Dhaka and was escorted from his airplane down a red carpet by Bangladeshi guards-of-honor.**

The United States is a major contributor of humanitarian aid to Bangladesh. U.S.-sponsored economic and food aid programs, in fact, began not long after the 1971 Liberation War. Today, the United States works with Bangladesh on long-term development projects relating to agriculture, nutrition, family planning, health, and rural employment. The United States, Bangladesh, and nongovernmental organizations (NGOs) work together to ensure that resources and aid are properly distributed.

In March 1991, a devastating cyclone struck Bangladesh, and the United States reponded with disaster relief support. The efforts of one U.S. Naval task force saved as many as 200,000 lives. In 1998, when Bangladesh experienced its worst flooding in the twentieth century, the United Sates donated large quantities of food and money to help the country recover.

Today, the United States is especially supportive of the proposal to build a gas pipeline between Bangladesh and India because the project, to which Bangladesh has yet to agree, could help boost Bangladesh's impoverished economy by attracting increased foreign investment in the country. U.S. officials and businesspeople are hopeful that the project will not only lead to a better economy and, therefore, better standards of living for the Bangladeshi people, but also to improved relations with India.

Fighting Terrorism Together

Bangladesh is committed to fighting worldwide terrorism and works closely with the United States to support this cause. Bangladesh was among the first to join the global coalition against terrorism after September 11, 2001, when the United States was struck by several acts of terrorism, including the dramatic crashing of two commercial passenger planes into the World Trade Center in New York City. The United States linked the terrorist incidents to the Al-Qaeda network, which was based in Afghanistan, and launched a military campaign into the country. Although Osama bin Laden, the leader of Al-Qaeda, has not yet been found, the Taliban, the iron-fisted government that hosted Al-Qaeda, was overthrown and the terrorist organization's activities were disrupted. Many countries, including Bangladesh, promised economic aid and disaster relief to help Afghanistan recover from the war. Bangladeshi prime minister Begum Khaleda Zia offered assistance in reconstructing Afghanistan, especially in the area of education for girls, which the Taliban prohibited.

The U.S. ambassador to Bangladesh Mary Ann Peters held talks with various local Muslim groups in Bangladesh after the terrorist events of September 11, 2001 to stress the importance of mutual communication and understanding of each other's cultures and differences. Following the talks, programs aimed at reducing religious prejudice and intolerance through dialogue

Left: **U.S. congressmen Joseph F. Crowley (*right*) and James A. McDermott (*left*) and U.S. ambassador to Bangladesh Mary Ann Peters (*center*) share a light-hearted moment during a press conference held in January 2002.**

were soon implemented to encourage peaceful solutions to potential disputes. Through Peters's actions, special arrangements were also made to take local Muslim religious leaders to various U.S. development assistance projects in Bangladesh. It was hoped that by viewing the fruits of the U.S.-led aid programs, which were working in the areas of agriculture, health, family planning, education, and technology, Bangladeshi religious leaders would be convinced that U.S. efforts in the country were sincere and that religion and differing belief systems did not have to get in the way of helping ordinary Bangladeshis better their lives.

The U.S. embassy in Dhaka has hosted seminars on topics such as religion, security, and justice and has even invited U.S.-based Islamic scholars to Bangladesh to speak. The U.S. embassy has also been trying to encourage faculty exchanges, joint research projects, and student exchange programs between Bangladeshi and American universities. Another current project is the creation of a forum between Bangladeshi and U.S. Islamic leaders. The forum is aimed at developing tolerance between the two countries and their respective religious followers and also providing Bangladeshi and U.S. Islamic leaders with a platform to speak openly and peacefully.

Bangladeshi and U.S. cooperation in the global campaign against terrorism also involves joint military training. In 2002, the two countries cohosted a military exercise in which twenty-two countries, including India, Nepal, France, and Japan, participated.

U.S.-Bangladesh Trade Relations

Bangladesh and the United States have a strong trade partnership. Most notably, the United States is a major importer of clothing produced in Bangladeshi garment factories, as well as processed jute, which is used to make the backing of carpets. The United States has been Bangladesh's largest customer for jute products, including burlap and carpet backing, since Bangladesh gained independence.

The U.S. embassy and the U.S. Trade Commission in Bangladesh have been actively encouraging trade and investment between the two countries by identifying and assisting U.S. companies that are suitable for joint projects in Bangladesh. Established in 1996, the American Chamber of Commerce (AmCham) in Bangladesh and the U.S. embassy also sponsor several trade shows a year. During these shows, businesspeople from both countries gather to promote their products and services to interested parties. These shows not only increase U.S. trade and investment in Bangladesh, but also give Bangladeshi businesspeople the opportunity to see U.S. products and services and learn about the latest technologies, goods, and services available in the United States.

Left: The relentless war between the two cola giants has entered even rural Bangladesh.

Left: **On April 2, 2002, David Kilgour, the Canadian secretary of state for Asia and the Pacific, addressed members of the press as part of his three-day visit to Bangladesh.**

U.S. exports to Bangladesh include wheat, fertilizers, cotton, airplanes, and medical supplies. About 40 percent of the garments Bangladesh exports are sold to the United States. Bangladesh, however, produces only about 10 percent of the export-quality cloth used by its garment industry. The expensive machinery used to make textiles is imported into the country. Importing cloth and machinery slows the growth of the Bangladeshi garment industry. It is hoped that increased foreign investments will lead to a brighter future for the Bangladeshi garment industry.

Canada-Bangladesh Trade Relations

Trade between Canada and Bangladesh has been steady, although figures from 2001 and 2002 show some decline. Canada's main exports to Bangladesh include grains, lentils and beans, and electrical equipment. Bangladesh, on the other hand, exports clothing, frozen fish, handicrafts, and ceramics to Canada. In 2001, Canadian exports to Bangladesh amounted to about CAN $130 million, while Bangladesh sold nearly CAN $190 million worth of goods to Canada. In 2002, Canadian exports to Bangladesh fell by about half, to about CAN $66.6 million, but imports from Bangladesh fell relatively slightly to CAN $164 million. The Export Development Corporation of Canada is one of several Canadian organizations that has been funding development projects in Bangladesh.

North Americans in Bangladesh

The North Americans in Bangladesh are mostly government officials, businesspeople, and aid workers. A U.S. embassy and an office of the High Commission of Canada are both located in Dhaka. Many U.S.-based missionary groups also operate in Bangladesh. Some have set up facilities known as "specialty hospitals," which are dedicated to children, patients with specific diseases, or the seriously or terminally ill.

CARE and Save the Children are two of the many aid organizations working in Bangladesh. North Americans working for these two organizations are usually involved in development work in rural villages, where they help people to start small businesses that will help spur the economy or train them in number of areas, such as livestock management, computer technology, and primary school education.

The Peace Corps

Volunteers for the Peace Corps of the United States first served in Bangladesh from 1961 to 1965, when it was called East Pakistan. In 1998, Peace Corps volunteers returned to independent Bangladesh after an absence of more than thirty years. Today, more than fifty Peace Corps volunteers work in Bangladesh, with most involved in education. They teach English and help develop educational resource centers for communities around the country. They also work with

Left: In September 1996, the "Green Umbrella" campaign, a reproductive health program, was launched in Bangladesh. Here, a panel of speakers that includes government representatives and community leaders waits to address a crowd before them.

Left: **U.S. ambassador to Bangladesh Mary Ann Peters (*left*) and Assistant Secretary of State for South Asian Affairs Christina B. Rocca (*right*) address participants in a press conference held in Dhaka in March 2002. Rocca became the head of the Bureau of South Asian Affairs in May 2001. The bureau and USAID are two divisions of the U.S. Department of State that are actively involved in improving relations between Bangladesh and the United States.**

teenagers at government-sponsored Youth Development Centers, at which young Bangladeshis can learn skills such as how to use computers and how to drill wells.

USAID

The United States Agency for International Development (USAID) has programs in Bangladesh relating to health, family planning, agriculture, disaster management, education, business, and democracy. USAID also works closely with the Bangladeshi government and with nongovernmental organizations (NGOs) on different projects that monitor elections to ensure credibility, promote human rights, and protect the rights of workers. USAID's programs in Bangladesh serve U.S. global interests by working toward stabilizing world population, eliminating hunger, protecting human health, promoting environmentally responsible growth, and providing humanitarian assistance in times of disaster.

Voluntary Service Overseas Canada (VSO)

Canadians volunteers serve in the Voluntary Service Overseas (VSO), which works in education, health, and rural development. Volunteers work alongside other agencies on projects that promote primary education, agriculture (including livestock development), and health care. Projects include libraries, teaching women to read, early learning centers, programs for small businesses, and participation in the World Health Organization-sponsored Polio Eradication Project.

Bangladeshis in North America

Bangladeshis come to North America for many reasons. While some seek employment, higher education, or better medical treatment, others arrive as tourists or visitors of family members who have immigrated to the United States or Canada.

Bangladeshis working in North America are mainly employed in the business, education, and health-care sectors. Often, they aspire to better lives for themselves and their families, who may live in North America or Bangladesh. Many are employed as professors, schoolteachers, and nurses, among other professions. Bangladeshi immigrants generally enjoy a good reputation in their new countries as friendly and hardworking people who are eager to contribute to their new homelands.

In 2001, more than 230,000 Bangladeshi-Americans were estimated to be living in the United States, with the largest communities in New York, New Jersey, California, and Texas.

Below: **Panna is one of several restaurants in New York City that serves Bangladeshi food. These restaurants usually serve a combination of Northern and Southern Indian food, as well as Bangladeshi or Pakistani food.**

Left: **First-year students at Bard College, Saiful Islam (*left*), who is from Bangladesh, and Sheena Ray (*center*), who is from Colorado, discuss their research procedures with Dr. Valeri Thomson (*right*) in 2000. Many well-to-do Bangladeshi families send their children to North America to pursue higher education.**

Bangladeshis living and working in the United States contribute not only to the workforce and economy of the country, but also to its cultural diversity. Bangladeshi-Americans, who include both new immigrants to the United States and U.S. citizens with a Bangladeshi heritage, are generally enthusiastic about preserving their culture. As a group, they act to educate non-Bangladeshis who live in the United States about Bangladeshi culture. Famous Bangladeshis in the United States include the late Dr. Fazlur Rahman Khan (1929–1982), who was the architectural engineer who designed the John Hancock Center and the Sears Tower, both in Chicago, Illinois. Khan also invented structural systems that are still used today.

Nearly one million Canadians have family ties to South Asia, including many with ties to Bangladesh. Most Bangladeshi immigrant families undergo a period of intense adjustment before adapting to their new lives in Canada. Apart from programs sponsored by the Canadian government to help these immigrants adapt, some areas also have small, established communities of Bangladeshis who tend to welcome newcomers with warmth, support, and a strong sense of their home country. Typical Bangladeshi families that have established themselves in Canada are bilingual, speaking both English and Bangla.

THE BANGLADESHI CONNECTION

Bangladeshi associations scattered throughout North America not only provide support among fellow Bangladeshis but also work to preserve and celebrate the Bangladeshi cultural identity through activities such as hosting a "Bangladesh Day" every year. The Internet has also helped Bangladeshis in North America keep in contact with one another and form community networks.

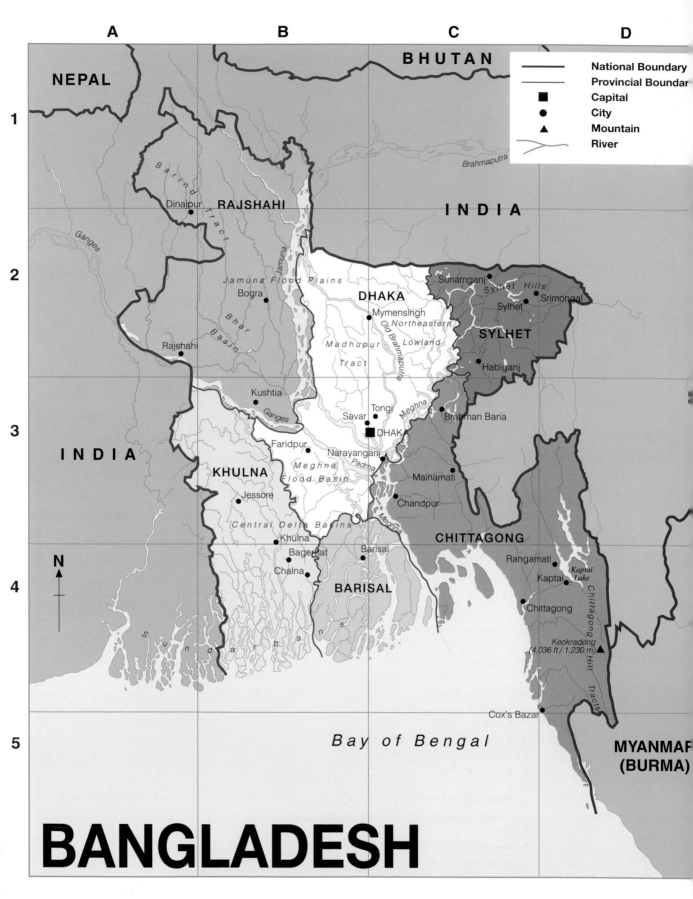

A   B   C   D

BHUTAN

		National Boundary
		Provincial Boundar
■		Capital
●		City
▲		Mountain
～～		River

NEPAL

Brahmaputra

1

Barind Tract

Dinajpur

RAJSHAHI

I N D I A

Ganges

Jamuna

2

Jamuna Flood Plains

Bogra

Sunamganj

Sylhet Hills

Srimongal

DHAKA

Sylhet

Bhar Basin

Mymensingh

Northeastern

SYLHET

Rajshahi

Old Brahmaputra

Madhupur Tract

Lowland

Habiganj

Kushtia

Ganges

Tongi

Meghna

3

Savar

Brahman Baria

I N D I A

Faridpur

■ DHAKA

Meghna
Flood Basin

Narayanganj

Padma

KHULNA

Mainamati

Jessore

Chandpur

Central Delta Basins

Meghna

CHITTAGONG

Khulna

Bagerhat

Barisal

Rangamati

Kaptai Lake

N

Chalna

BARISAL

Kaptai

4

S u n d a r b a n s

Chittagong

Chittagong Hill Tracts

Keokradong
(4,036 ft / 1,230 m) ▲

Cox's Bazar

5

Bay of Bengal

MYANMAR
(BURMA)

BANGLADESH

Above: Rickshaw riders often park outside busy market areas to wait for potential customers.

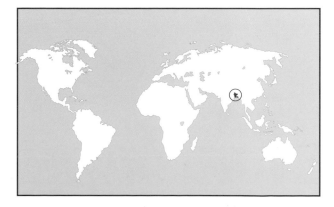

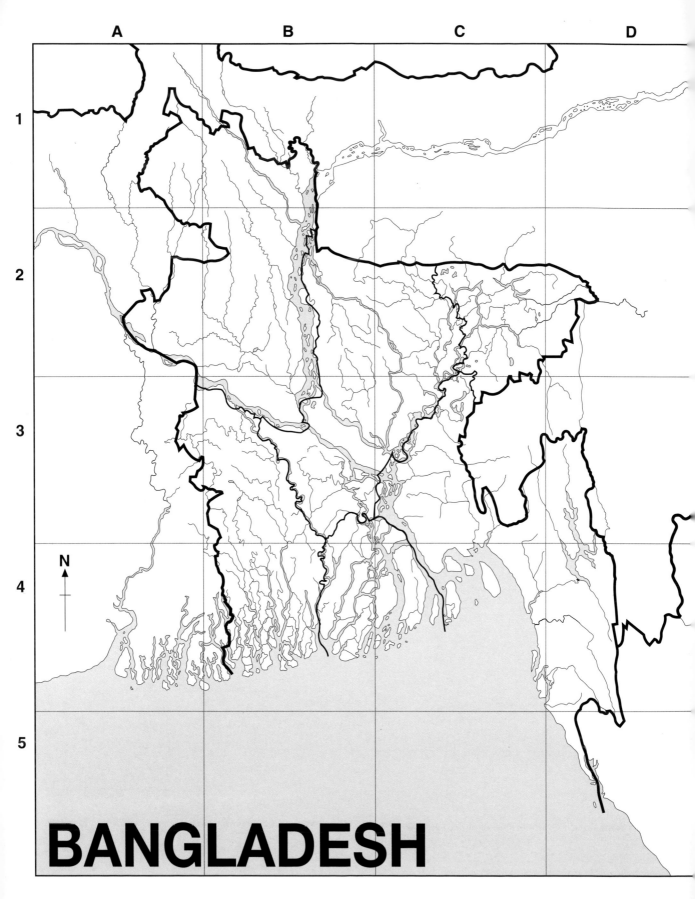

BANGLADESH

How Is Your Geography?

Learning to identify the main geographical areas and points of a country can be challenging. Although it may seem difficult at first to memorize the locations and spellings of major cities or the names of mountain ranges, rivers, deserts, lakes, and other prominent physical features, the end result of this effort can be very rewarding. Places you previously did not know existed will suddenly come to life when referred to in world news, whether in newspapers, television reports, other books and reference sources, or on the Internet. This knowledge will make you feel a bit closer to the rest of the world, with its fascinating variety of cultures and physical geography.

This map can be duplicated for use in a classroom. (PLEASE DO NOT WRITE IN THIS BOOK!) Students can then fill in any requested information on their individual map copies. The student can also make a copy of the map and use it as a study tool to practice identifying place names and geographical features on his or her own.

Above: **Four Bangladeshi children travel along a river in a small wooden boat.**

Bangladesh at a Glance

Official Name	People's Republic of Bangladesh
Capital	Dhaka
Official Language	Bangla (Bengali)
Population	133,376,684 (July 2002 estimate)
Land Area	55,584 square miles (144,000 square km)
Divisions	Barisal, Chittagong, Dhaka, Khulna, Rajshahi, Sylhet
Highest Point	Keokradong, 4,036 feet (1,230 m)
Coastline	360 miles (580 km)
Major Cities	Chittagong, Khulna, Cox's Bazar, Sylhet, Dhaka
Major Rivers	Brahmaputra-Jamuna, Ganges-Padma, Meghna
Major Festivals	*Eid-ul-Fitr*, *Eid-ul-Azha*, *Durga Puga*, *Buddha Purnima*
Secular Holidays	International Mother Language Day (February 21), Independence Day (March 26), Victory Day (December 16)
Famous Leaders	Sheikh Mujibur Rahman (Sheikh Mujib)
	Major General Zia ur Rahman
	Lieutenant General Hussain Muhammad Ershad
	Begum Khaleda Zia ur Rahman
	Sheikh Hasina Wajed
National Anthem	*Amar Sonar Bangla* (My Golden Bengal)
Major Exports	Clothes, frozen seafood, jute, leather, tea
Major Imports	Building materials, chemicals, coal, electrical appliances, food and food products, machinery, petroleum, textiles, transportation equipment
Currency	Taka (58 Taka = U.S. $1 as of 2003)

Opposite: **This aerial view of a vegetable market shows the diversity of crops grown in Bangladesh.**

Glossary

Bangla Vocabulary

ashraf (AH-shrahf): a small, elite class of Muslim Bangladeshis.

atraf (AH-trahf): ordinary Muslim Bangadeshis who form the larger, lower social class.

alpana (AHL-poh-nah): a form of painting that uses a rice powder mixture as paint.

badhia (BAD-ee-ah): people who live on boats.

banshi (BAH-shee): a flute.

baul (BAH-ul): a type of folk music.

bede (BEH-deh): an alternative name for badhia.

bharatnatyam (BHAH-raht-naht-yah): a type of Bangladeshi classical dance.

biryani (BIH-rih-yah-nih): a popular rice dish that combines many ingredients.

botni (BOHT-nih): a prayer mat.

burkha (BOHR-kah): a long, black gown that some Muslim women wear to cover their entire bodies, except for the eyes, hands, and feet.

cha (CHAH): tea.

cholito bhasha (CHOH-lih-toh bhah-shah): colloquial, or everyday, Bangla.

daal (DAAHL): a thick lentil soup.

dhole (DHOHL): wooden drums

dotara (DOH-tah-rah): a four-stringed instrument used in folk music.

dudh bhat (DOODH bhaht): a breakfast dish of cooked rice mixed with either milk or water and date palm sugar.

dupata (doh-PAH-tah): a large shawl.

gur (GURH): date palm sugar.

hajj (HAWJ): an annual pilgrimage to Mecca that all Muslims try to make at least once in their lives.

jamdani (JAHM-dah-nee): a fabric that has been described as "woven air" because of its near see-through quality.

jari (JAH-ree): a type of folk music.

jatra (JAH-trah): a type of folk drama in which traditional myths and folklore are acted out.

jumma (JOO-mah): the collective name of Bangladesh's tribal peoples.

Kabaddi (KAH-bah-dih): Bangladesh's national sport; a game resembling tag.

kalajam (KAH-loh-jahm): a dessert that is milk, sugar, flour, and ghee.

kathak (KOH-thohk): a type of Bangladeshi classical dance.

khali (KHAH-lee): empty.

korma (KOR-mah): a mildly spicy curry.

kula (KUH-lah): a flat and horseshoe-shaped basket.

lassi (LAHS-sih): a yogurt drink.

lunghi (LUNGE): a sarong, or skirt, worn by Bangladeshi men.

madrasas (mah-DRAH-shahs): Islamic religious schools.

mandap (MAWN-dohp): a tree of life.

mandara (MAHN-dah-rah): small cymbals.

marfati (MAH-for-tee): a type of Bangladeshi folk music.

mishti doi (MEESH-tee doy): sweetened yogurt; a Bangladeshi dessert.

naan (NAHN): a type of flat bread.

nakshi kantha (NOHK-shee KAHN-thah): finely embroidered quilts.

padma (POD-mah): lotus.

pantabhat (PAHN-tah-bhaht): a breakfast dish consisting of rice that has been slightly fermented in water.

parata (POH-rah-tah): a type of flat bread.

Patuagan (POH-too-ah-gahn): the ancient art of storytelling that involves dramatizing a story that has been depicted on a painted scroll.

pitha (PEE-thah): types of pastries that can be either fried, baked, or boiled.

poribar (POH-ree-bahr): the traditional basic family unit in Bangladesh consisting of a man, his wife, their unmarried children, their married sons, and the families of their married sons.

purdah (PAWR-dah): the Islamic practice of physically separating men and women after they have reached puberty.

rasgolla (RAWSH-oh-goh-lah): a white-colored dessert made from milk, sugar, and cream of wheat.

rickshaw mysteri dokan (RIK-shah MEES-tree DOH-kahn): a rickshaw shop.

rickshaw wallah (RIK-shah WAH-lah): a rickshaw driver.

ruti (ROO-tee): a round, flat bread.

Salaam aleykum (sah-LAAM ah-LIE-koom): a greeting Muslim Bangladeshis use when they meet that means "Peace be unto you."

shadhu bhasha (SHAHD-hu bhah-shah): formal or literary Bangla.

shokher hari (SHOK-her HAH-rih): a special terra-cotta pot reserved mainly for special occasions, such as weddings.

shora (SHAW-rah): a uniquely shaped terra-cotta lid for cooking pots that curves upward from edge to center.

samosas (sah-MOH-sahs): deep-fried thin pastries filled with spicy mixtures of various vegetables or meat.

sandesh (SHOHN-dehs): a dessert made from milk, sugar, nuts, and cardamom.

shalwar kameez (SAH-loh-ahr kah-MEEZ): a type of women's outfit consisting of baggy pants and a loose tunic top.

shapla (SHAH-PLAH): water lily; the national flower of Bangladesh.

sitalpati (SHEE-tohl-pah-tih): a special type of mat woven out of cane that has been soaked in water.

tarkari (TAWR-kah-ree): curries.

thana (THAH-nah): groups of villages that are subdivisions of districts.

zilla (JEH-lah): districts.

zorda (JORH-dah): a dessert made from sweetened cooked rice and nuts.

English Vocabulary

advocated: publicly supported or recommended.

animistic: having the belief that all aspects of the natural environment, including natural objects, such as rocks, contain spirits that can do good or evil and be worshipped.

doctrines: guiding principles or teachings.

ensemble: a group of musicians performing together.

sanitation: the disposal of sewage and solid waste.

sitar: a lute originating from India that has a small, pear-shaped body and a long, broad neck.

tabla: a small hand drum that can be tuned to different pitches.

More Books to Read

The 100 Greatest Disasters of All Time. Stephen J. Spignesi (Citadel Press)

American Islam: Growing Up Muslim in America. Richard Wormser (Walker & Co.)

Bangladesh. Cultures of the World series. Mariam Whyte (Marshall Cavendish)

Bangladesh. Enchantment of the World series. Jason Laure (Children's Book Press)

Banker to the Poor: Micro-lending and the Battle Against World Poverty. Muhammad Yunus with Alan Jolis (Aurum Press)

The Ganges. Great Rivers of the World series. David Cumming (World Almanac)

Land of the Tiger: A Natural History of the Indian Subcontinent. Valmik Thapur (University of California Press)

The Man-Eating Tigers of Sundarbans. Sy Montgomery (Houghton Mifflin)

Meyebela: My Bengali Girlhood. Taslima Nasrin (Steerforth Press)

Selected Poems. Rabindranath Tagore (South Asia Books)

Stolen Dreams. David L. Parker, Robert Conrow, Lee Engfer, and Leeann Engfer (Lerner Publications)

Videos

Concert for Bangladesh. (Paramount Studio)

Credit Where Credit is Due. (Bullfrog Films)

From Docklands to Dhaka. (Bullfrog Films)

Web Sites

www.alldesi.net/fun/sports/kabaddi.htm

www.bangladeshgov.org/

www.grameen-info.org

www.webpak.net/~ricksha/

Due to the dynamic nature of the Internet, some web sites stay current longer than others. To find additional web sites, use a reliable search engine with one or more of the following keywords to help you locate information about Bangladesh. Keywords: *Bengal, Chittagong, Cox's Bazar, Dhaka, Ganges, Grameen Bank, Jamuna, Padma, Sundarbans.*

Index